The Boys of St. Columb's

THE BOYS OF ST. COLUMB'S

'... They would banish the conditional
forever, this generation ...'

Maurice Fitzpatrick

The Liffey Press

Published by
The Liffey Press
Ashbrook House, 10 Main Street
Raheny, Dublin 5, Ireland
www.theliffeypress.com

A catalogue record of this book is
available from the British Library.

ISBN 978-1-905785-77-3

This book is based on the television programme "The Boys of
St. Columb's" produced by Maccana Teoranta and West Park Pictures

Printed in the United Kingdom by J.F. Print.

Contents

To Marina

Introduction

Some of the eight men chronicled in this book have been life-long friends; some have been colleagues; others hardly know each other; others still have had uneasy relations throughout their lives. They were all born between the years 1933 and 1947. They were all beneficiaries of the Education Act passed in Northern Ireland in 1947. This Act made grammar school education free for any student who passed its auxiliary test known as the Eleven Plus. They all attended St. Columb's College, a Catholic boys, diocesan school in Derry City. Thus they form a generation and, in some respects, a coterie. The education they received in the school, academically good in itself, has the added interest of bridging two eras: the dark post-war years and the liberal sixties. The thesis of this book is that they form as fine an example as exists of the watershed in Irish history brought about by that educational overhaul. Other examples throughout Northern Ireland can be found, but my concern here is to examine its impact through the lens of St. Columb's (where it had a concentrated effect) in order to understand its province-wide influence. Many of the interviewees speak of having 'broken' the Northern Irish State, modifying unionist domination in Northern Ireland. The narrative reveals itself discretely through the words of the eight participants. I am part compiler of their testimonies, part arranger of the history and part story-teller.

On my first trip to the building of the former St. Columb's, I learn what remains of the original school building: the vista from the front gate is the same. From the top floor, looking on to that gate, the view is much the same except that the handball alley is now a bus bay. The library is excellent with winding banisters and views of three sides of the college. It was mainly used by priests who had brought back artifacts from the missions: a duck-billed platypus or a Maori shield. They studied them

1

there. Today the GAA pitch has become a soccer pitch and it is now adjacent to the school's front, whereas in the 1950s the playing fields were parallel. The dormitories upstairs are now classrooms. The stained glass of the church and the church itself is generally the same. The altar has changed slightly. The school overlooks the Catholic Bogside on one side, the Protestant Fountain on the other side. In the 1950s and 1960s the former was ghettoised; the latter besieged. St. Columb's was a small area – two or three acres – between them. St. Columb's is now located on Buncrana Road and this, its original site, has become another school, Lumen Christi.

Patrick O'Doherty, principal of Lumen Christi, has given many tours to past pupils returning to the original site of St. Columb's College for the first time in thirty or forty years. Their reactions are clear and lacking in ambivalence. Either the man breaks down and almost cries at the powerful memories that come to him, or all his bitterness comes to the surface. Reactions are always polarised, never middle-of-the-road.

I first became aware of the Boys of St. Columb's twelve years ago, in 1998. A teacher in my secondary school announced that John Hume had just won the Nobel Prize for Peace. He also said that Seamus Heaney, winner of the 1995 Nobel Prize for Literature, had gone to the same school. My teacher went on to say 'they still talk about the English teacher they had in school. He must have been a wonderful teacher to have educated such men'. Twelve years on, I try to piece together what that snippet of information meant to me. It certainly stayed with me

2

that two of Ireland's most recent Nobelists sat at the feet of a master who might have been instrumental in shaping their lives. I now know that his name was S.B. O'Kelly. He has loomed large in the consciousness of many of his pupils all their lives.

As a student of English literature at university, I read Seamus Deane. Strange to say that his novel about growing up in Derry, *Reading in the Dark*, did not immediately make a strong impression on me. But even stranger, I went back to read it again and again. Why did I become more fascinated with it each time? There was something in Derry that I wanted to explore. The more I researched the city, the more Deane's novel, and other things too, made sense to me.

I wondered what made Catholics realise their plight and how they felt being obstructed and also curiously enabled (I am thinking about free education) by the British state. I wondered what Sharkey and Brady, university roommates in the Republic, spoke about in the late sixties. What did Heaney and Deane, classmates and literary mates, who 'went up to Belfast' to study in Queen's at the end of the fifties, discuss? What drove Phil Coulter when he left university and went to London to become a famous musician? And how was it for Eamonn McCann and John Hume to return, educated at third level, to the Bogside in the late 1960s?

In February 2007 Seamus Deane was kind enough to give me an interview in Dublin for a journal in Japan. He spoke candidly about the journey he had made. Sitting there, with my dictaphone running, listening to his answers to my questions about the history of the state, it occurred to me that I must have been sitting in much the place as Sean O'Mordha when he directed his intriguing documentary, *The Seven Ages* [of the Irish State]. Light that was spilling in through the window was of a piece with the natural light used by O'Mordha in his documentary. The building where I sat was the site where James Joyce read his famous lecture on Ibsen ('Drama and Life' on 20 January 1900). It is Newman House, named after the founder of the National Catholic University. From Deane's office, two enormous windows look out over the Iveagh Gardens. St Stephen's Green South is on the other side of the building. I asked him:

'You couldn't have been aware in St. Columb's in the 1950s that you were part of a generation – yourself, Seamus Heaney and John Hume (although Hume was a few years older) and others – that would make a huge impact in Ireland and further afield. Nonetheless, you personally must have been aware that you were one of the first from the Bogside to get as far as university. Is that so?

Yes, I guess I must have been, yeah ... It was the first generation coming through. The concept of getting free secondary education – because then what we paid in St. Columb's was three pounds, ten shillings a year for books. That was the only school expense. But apart from the fact that you weren't out working at fourteen it meant, for a start, that you weren't bringing money into the house. Anyway in Derry you wouldn't have got a job, there weren't any jobs to be had so you were as well to go to school. And my parents were very anxious that we should do this ... And they actually recognised that a cohort of Catholic kids going to school was what was going to break the Northern Irish State. And it wasn't that obvious to me when I was ten or eleven. But I was sort of educated into this by Eamonn McCann who was, what, two years behind me? One or two. He went to the same school. And he was the worst footballer I have ever seen. He was even worse than Heaney. And I was a good footballer. But we'd play a bit of football after school and sometimes Eamonn and I would sit on the railings, talking politics. And every so often I'd get down and thump the ball into the centre of the field and then get back up on the railings again. It was that kind of really professional football ... His father and my father were best friends. He and I weren't best friends, but we had conversations and we were acquaintances at school. But I found him too embarrassing on the football field to be associated with' (*Journal of Irish Studies*, Japan, Vol. 21).

I see now that that answer prompted me to script the documentary. It told me many things. Firstly, I had learned that the firebrand and magnetic Eamonn McCann also went to the college: I knew now that not one or two, but a group of very talented boys came through St. Columb's at that time. The generation – 'a generation who had seen a sign!', in Seamus Heaney's words – grasped education with both hands. Secondly, I knew too that they played football together, with varying degrees of ability. The football field seems to have been the equivalent of a mosque where inciters gathered to talk politics. If it is unusual for eleven-year-olds to talk about instigating social change, then surely the times too were unusual. Out of this crucible, a vision of a more robust Catholic identity in Northern Ireland grew. Thirdly, as I was growing up and watching news reports on Ulster television – as unremittingly bleak a news programme as has ever been broadcast – I got a notion of the North. But it was a warped notion. It was too caught up in the minutiae of daily atrocities. The whole place was associated with terrorism and politics – terrorists who wanted to control the province and politicians who failed to do the same. Later, studying for the Leaving Certificate, I was still more confounded by political gestures: Terence O'Neill hosted Sean Lemass in Stormont (January 1965) and Lemass reciprocated in Dublin a month later. I memorised it all by rote. There was, however, history to be understood that neither vapid glad-handing nor news reports of carnage could teach.

All these unorganised ideas needed composition into an intelligible structure. That happened when Deane said to me, 'a cohort of Catholic kids going to school was what was going to break the Northern Irish State'. The Northern Irish State thus became differentiated in my mind to the one I had learned about in books or had seen on television. That Northern Ireland, hemmed in on one side by water and, on the other, by the 1922 partition, still existed. The Northern Ireland of division and segregated schooling more or less exists today. But Deane's words went further back, pre-dating the civil unrest of the late 1960s, reaching to the Derry of his childhood. The Northern Irish State to him was tangled up with all manner of oppressions, deprivations, a community which had turned its hatred in upon itself, a place of doctrinaire separation. Derry, a town that was over 65 per cent Catholic, could not return a Catholic mayor at election time. It was inevitable that this situation would be dismantled due in large part to the coming of age of educated Catholics. It was a state in which the great threat to unionism was not a United Ireland but rather to concede that we are all the same.

The history of this era (approximately 1922–1968) has unfortunately been eclipsed by the focus in the media on 'the Troubles' (1968–1998). It is unfortunate because the three decades of the Troubles were not inevitable, as an examination of the causes of the 1960s conflict between unionists and nationalists shows. The long war of attack and

reprisal teaches us little. The train of events that led to it illustrates the real conflict and divide that lies at the heart of the province. Only an examination of that history can make a small contribution towards an approach to understanding critical developments of that time. This book is intended as a contribution to that history.

Moving from textbook history to history in the concrete, a history of an identity, my project was to engage with the slow-burn of history and to show how ideas modify society. This version of history gave the lie to the other history – what is written in textbooks – which marks events and dates and does not register the gradual shifts in society nearly enough. To pose the question: what measure of success that the participants had do we ascribe to St. Columb's? Why is it that four of the eight participants started their lives as school teachers, married young and yet chose to go much further in their respective fields? That was the history, the history of their generation, I wanted to examine. The revolutionary spirit that prevailed in the 1960s was surely a contributing factor in fracturing the Orange state; mass media played its part; a misguided and craven British security policy also played a role. But I kept falling back on the Educational Act of 1947. The British Government extended this right to a Catholic minority who were otherwise divested of so many rights. Unionists had to ratify it because, since the legislation came from the 'mainland', they were under duress to accept it. Terence O'Neill argued in Stormont Government buildings that unionists must not let a good act of legislation be 'wrecked upon the rocks of religious controversy'. Many unionists possibly hoped that those Catholics who did see an education through could be absorbed into the present system and the status quo would remain. They did not envisage ghettos like the Bogside producing such fine and determined minds. A professional class rose in a single generation which provided leadership and confidence for generations to come. Even if the Catholic populace happened to be defeated on occasion, there was a glimpse of a new reality for anyone who stayed on at school. Professionals would not accept the cynical oppression that had been the lot of Catholics up to that point.

Growing up in a border county, I was also dismayed at how complacent the South has become about partition. With every generation, the perception of the North as 'other' grows sharper in the Republic. That the Troubles have ended has done little to stanch this tendency. Alienation between the two states grows apace. Ask a young person from the South where Limavady or Ballymoney is and they'll likely not know; but they will know it is in the North. This alienation is a result of an unconscious acceptance of a divided Ireland by the majority of people in the Republic.

On the surface, there is little reason why I should have come to this story. I was born two miles south, on the 'other' side of the border. Derry is not my town and, putting so much distance between Ireland and myself in relocating to Japan, it was a surprising twist in my life that I began researching it. (It put me in mind of Hamlet's bafflement: 'What's Hecuba to him, or he to Hecuba, that he should weep for her?' But the Derry Hecuba was implacably the subject of my thoughts night and day for two years.) The history of Derry and the life trajectories of its luminaries bear some resemblance to the societal makeup of Japan. Japan had been, during its Edo period (1600–1867), a strictly stratified society along the lines of a pyramid: lords at the top, then samurai, farmers and merchants at the bottom. The opening up of schools and universities to western ideas and the redistribution of land changed that. In researching St. Columb's, I subconsciously applied my understanding of the structure of Japanese society in the Middle Ages where a modern society emerged quickly.

I read Japanese history in the light of Northern Ireland, which seemed so time-lagged before 1947. Certainly a reading of Japanese history shows the deeply unsettling effect that modernity had on feudal precedent, causing a war and a change of capital city which is suggestive of the North. I see the two communities in the North after the 1947 Education Act somehow representing strains of the same clash. The Catholic people, who were oppressed, found through education a means of establishing equality; and the Protestant people, who had held power, found this challenge shocking and unsettling. But, as with the coming of modernity in Japan, the trend towards a more equitable society was irreversible despite determined opposition.

The South, having dispelled colonial occupation in 1921, came to take certain rights for granted which in the North had to be contested. Eamonn McCann's account of an Irish teacher in the Bogside of his youth illustrates this (*War and an Irish Town*). The teacher was interned without trial for speaking his own language in Belfast, finally released to attend his mother's funeral and subsequently left the North forever. Derry is a town with three of its four limbs pointing towards Donegal. It is wedded to the old culture that Donegal represents. To this day, sessions of music with Donegal-Irish ballads are common in Derry. Yet when Bogsiders met their Donegal counterparts, in St. Columb's College for example, they realised that their two governments had forced a wedge between them. Donegal boarders, being from the South, had to pay fees at St. Columb's and had no experience of a state that antagonised them on tribal grounds. They had been taught the language of their ancestors and found, when they met the denizens of Derry City, that the boys were liable to be bullied by the police yet were beneficiaries of a superior social welfare system. What Donegal culture represented to Derry City people and what it meant to Donegal natives were often two quite different things.

A major concern of mine has always been to try to read the springs of an individual's talent from the time and place they emerge. Interviewing Anthony Cronin in 2005, one of my questions concerned his time as an *Irish Times* columnist during the 1970s and 1980s. He told me:

'I called the na gCopaleen book the ...'

'*Life and Times*.'

'*The Life and Times* and I think that's an important aspect of it. A lot of your questions, Maurice, for example, have been about the effects of the times on the writer and I want to get that right for people.' (*Journal of Irish Studies,* Japan, Vol. 20)

After working on *The Boys of St. Columb's,* which treats of a specific time and place, I learned a lot about trying to capture the essence of a certain era that interests me. While the individual talent of the people recorded in this account is undeniable, it is in their working through the struggles of the state they inherited that that talent came to full maturity.

I first met the man who would direct the film version of *The Boys of St. Columb's,* Tom Collins, in Tokyo. A Northern Ireland Film Festival took place there in February 2008 and the committee flew Tom out to publicise his hugely successful Irish language film, *Kings.* The following day I took him to Yasukunijinja, a controversial shrine in Tokyo which commemorates General Tojo and others who were a little right of centre. When Tom and I eventually sat down to discuss the film later that year, I pointed out that the theme of *Antigone* – the play of a woman who takes a principled stand but brings down chaos on her people as a result – was a central concern of some of the participants. It was also germane to the Field Day project, two of whose directors – Seamus Heaney and Seamus Deane – were in the film line-up. Tom liked *Antigone* both for its visual and thematic potential. It is at once tribal and mythic.

Deane had read *Antigone* as being a dramatisation of what was happening in the North, a moment when the North itself became a stage. Heaney said that an essay published by Conor Cruise O'Brien about the first civil rights march in Derry on 5 October 1968 caused the character Antigone to jump out of her box. Up to that point she had been a character in a classic play. Now she was a Derry woman just as much as she was Oedipus's daughter: 'It is not a propaganda play. It is a story of understanding that each side has got its necessary position to hold.' Heaney also spoke of the Nazi German production of *Antigone* and the Apartheid South African production – in which both sides of the audience felt that they were being vindicated when they witnessed *Antigone* on stage. Tom also liked the idea of a conversation between Deane and Heaney on these topics. So gradually we moved towards envisaging the film and entering production.

Derry seemed to me to be divided by the markings and lines of time: the Presbyterian, the Anglican, the Mason, the Protestant and the Catholic. It was a Protestant fort, the throughfare of the Presbyterian, with etchings of the Great War over the Protestant diamond. The Catholic terraced housing lay outside the walls of the besieged city. Their wall – the wall of Free Derry – faces the walls of the garrison city. While the men of Ulster were marching towards the Somme (1914-1918), a rebellion happened in Dublin. This is not commemorated in Derry.

This is the story of the Boys of St. Columb's, an example of the first generation of the Catholic masses to be educated in Northern Ireland. The Church Latin education they received was broad enough to feed the talents of parliamentarians, writers and musicians. Though this education was martinet, it was not taken for granted as it tends to be today. There was an awe about this education. Heaney wrote of his neighbours: 'Old men standing up to shake my hand ... Whispers informed strangers that I was the eldest/ Away at school.' The sacerdotal pause and whispering is apt. The priests at St. Columb's College would surely have looked on Heaney – a scholarship boy, hugely intelligent – as a potential priest. His neighbours' quiet deference comes from their expectations of him. The script of *The Boys of St. Columb's* came of the crucible of this pride, awe and dedication.

Each of the book's subjects has the ability to tell stories that take the viewer through their background and down the corridors of St.

Columb's. But what distinguishes their stories is their ability to
alter the perspective, to move
up to a hawk's-eye view and
set them against the backdrop
of international events: Deane
says that 1972 was the first
year that British manufacturing
showed a deficit in export, and
he reads this diminution of the
British economy in the light of
the intensification of its policy
in Northern Ireland; elsewhere,
Heaney speaks of Anahorish, his
primary school, being 'a kind of
nineteenth century school still

operating in the mid-twentieth'. McCann speaks of the population
pyramid of the Bogside resembling nineteenth century industrial England, rather than twentieth century Ireland. There are many linkages
of the archaic make-up of Northern Ireland and how the 'Eleven Plus
Generation' embodied the forces of modernity. Key dates in the history
of Derry and Northern Ireland – the 1947 Educational Act, the baton-
charging of the 1951 St. Patrick's Day parade inside the Walls of Derry,
the 1968 baton-charging of the first civil rights march in Derry and 30
January 1972 (Bloody Sunday) were tangible happenings on the streets,
in schools. What characterises the participants' narratives is that they
move comfortably between the concrete and the abstract.

There are several reasons why revolution happened in Derry in 1968:
the liberal hope, in evidence throughout the world then, that peaceful protest could effect change was also present in Derry; the incipient collapse of
Northern Irish industry; the clash of a new and confident generation of
Catholics within the fusty Unionist political structure. Each of these three
factors threatened the dominant trend of voting and it threatened the gerrymandered electoral system. With the decline of the heavy industries, the
business vote became much less secure. As Catholics had become broadly
educated, the Catholic middle class underwent a sea change. A new party
was born out of that mix, ultimately to be led by John Hume. Hume

had helped to form this party, the Social Democratic and Labour Party (SDLP). He retained his seat with ease and, going beyond party politics, he became a universally respected interpreter of Northern Irish politics for the rest of the world.

Now was an ideal time to make the film and write the book because a lot of valuable ground has been explored in Vinny Cunningham's seminal films *The Battle of the Bogside* and *No Go – The Free Derry Story*. The route has been paved, so to speak, for a full probing into why the Catholic body politic came to an increased awareness of their situation. Their campaign for full citizenship – jobs, houses and universal suffrage – happened at the end of the 1960s. This book suggests that the education boys received in a school such as St. Columb's was a chief source of the revolution, and examines the forces that alter people's concerns from exigencies of survival to a full consciousness of their political circumstances. The consequences of that monumental shift are still being felt today.

A large part of Eamonn McCann's excellent first book, *War and an Irish Town*, is devoted to history. It is worth bearing in mind that when McCann left St. Columb's he had learned enough Greek to read the great historian, Thucydides, in the original. Thus patterns of the past (in the minds of educated Catholics at the time) informed on events in Derry. McCann is a fervid supporter of learning the classics, believing that learning about Greece and Rome has a hugely formative effect on the young: 'I cannot see why anyone would not benefit from knowledge of Rome and Greece.' The Boys of St. Columb's were educated and they were able to absorb the course of international events – from Prague to Memphis. They were able to read the pattern of international events into the politics of home.

In the examination of the strictures which existed for Catholics and the chief force which brought about the change – education – I attempt to go to the source of the conflict to elucidate its solution. Catholics were lifted out of their second class mould by the Educational Act of 1947. The individuals profiled here form a pioneer group who went on to fulfill themselves. Some may cavil at the omission of St. Columb's' other famous sons, such as Brian Friel and Martin O'Neill. My only reply is that I was more concerned with the generation stated above than with chronicling every alumnus of St. Columb's.

Introduction

Although there was an archive fire at St. Columb's, none of the records of those who attended St. Columb's (b. 1946–1957) were lost. As Father Eamon Martin put it, they 'were all spared the flames'. I am grateful to the former St. Columb's College President, Father Eamon Martin, and to the present President, Sean McGinty; to the college archivist Bob McKimm; and to Dermot Carlin for their conversation and insights.

I would like to thank my first readers of the full text or part of the text – Ciaran Murray, John Dolan, Brendan McCann and James Sharkey – for giving so generously of their time and so enthusiastically of their encouragement. I am grateful to West Park Pictures and Macanna Teoranta for their role in making this tie-in book happen to compliment our documentary film. Thanks to: Mary Hayes and Shay, Festus Jennings, Lisa Hyde, the Okazaki family, the Nishimura family, the Kayou Club, Tom and Jane Hachey, Tony Doherty, Garbhan Downey, Robert Gwyn Palmer, Pat Hume, Peter Gallagher, Patrick Heaney, Hugh Heaney, Dan Heaney, Charlie Heaney, Eamon Deane, Gerard Deane, Sean McMahon, Vinny McCormack, Paddy Mullarky, Peter McDonald, Jude Collins, Micheal Collins, Colm Sharkey, The Sharkey family, Clive O'Brien, Richard Doherty, Cathal Logue, Patrick McGoldrick, Eddie Mahon, John Walsh, P.J. Doherty, Sean Quinn and the Quinn Group, Shane Connaghton, Seamus and Bernadette Fitzpatrick, Patrick O'Doherty, Patrick Mullarky, Margo Harkin, Maeve McAdam, Cllr. Helen Quigley and Mayor Gerard Diver. I thank Sean Quinn for the use of his helicopter during our aerial shoot in Derry. I thank the Cavan Arts Council for supporting me at the Tyrone Gutherie Centre. Thanks to Michael D'Arcy, the Japan-Ireland Association, the Japan Society of Trinity College and the Japanese Embassy to Ireland.

I heartily thank my colleagues at Keio University, Tokyo. And I thank the staff at Keio library – the repository in which I worked – for the manifold assistance I received.

Maurice Fitzpatrick
March 2010

Background/History

After the formal founding of the Northern Irish State, with the Government of Ireland Act (1920), unionists resorted more and more to the gerrymander to dominate the areas that had a Catholic majority. Since proportional representation did not serve their ends, they abolished it. An ineffectual, complacent single-party government – puppet of Westminster – ruled the North for the next half century. Gerrymandering first escalated in Derry when a Catholic was elected mayor in the eighteenth century for the first time since 1688. Inside the Guildhall in Derry the names of town councilors are written on the wall. In January 1920, Alderman Hugh C. O'Doherty managed to storm the citadel but the victory was pyrrhic: it intensified gerrymandering, ensuring that Protestants obtained political leverage disproportionate to their numbers. Guildhall unionists arranged that there would never be another Catholic mayor after that. It was to be the 1970s before the town returned another Catholic mayor. The formality of the gerrymander was hardly needed, given the make-up of the state. Derry, with its Catholic majority, was exceptional. Understandably, when the civil rights movement formed in Derry in 1968, the establishment of electoral reform (one man, one vote) was utmost on their agenda.

For all that, the Guildhall in Derry is replete with the history of both sides. Earl Hugh O'Donnell and St. Columb of Iona adorn the stained glass, side by side with figures of the British royalty.

Fermanagh Facts, a book published about the politics of County Fermanagh, is a good illustration of how discrimination in the North worked. If a Catholic and a Protestant both applied for a job in a school, post office, etc., the Protestant would get it. A Protestant stood a five or six times better chance than a Catholic of getting a job. Overarching this rigging of job allocation was the biased electoral system.

'The gerrymander works on a very simple principle: In the Unionist constituencies the Nationalist minority is made as large as possible, whereas the Unionist minority is made as small as possible. This ensured a maximum "waste" of Nationalist votes and a maximum utilisation of Unionist votes' (*Fermanagh Facts*, Fermanagh Civil Rights Association, p. 2).

Thus, in a county with a Catholic majority such as Fermanagh, constituency boundaries were drawn to ensure that South Fermanagh had a clearly nationalist majority and the other two constituencies – Enniskillen and Lisnaskea – had narrow unionist majorities. The two unionist constituencies could then always out-vote the nationalist one. This theoretical democracy perverted the course of all housing and job allocation. Gerrymandering also codified an electoral divide which endures to this day: Protestants will vote for a Protestant candidate and Catholics will vote for Catholics at elections. Gerrymandering as a mentality sadly persists today in some arenas.

Terence O'Neill is a pivotal figure in the historical background of this story. His political inclusivism such as his insistence on decency for Catholics, in his defence of the 1947 Education Act, twenty years later caused his political demise (at the hands of Paisley and his followers, who would subsequently be saboteurs of the Sunningdale Agreement). O'Neill's support for civil rights was the logical conclusion of his support for the Education Act. The civil rights movement itself flowed partly from the Education Act. It is also interesting to ponder that Hume, one of the architects of Sunningdale – the agreement which Ulster was to accept in essence decades of violence later – only received grammar school education because of the Education Act. This education was to be the vehicle through which Catholics could agitate for social decency.

Fossicking through boxes of archives, I learned that the reason St. Columb's is now relocated to Buncrana Road is because of gerrymandering. The school's population mushroomed – a consequence of the Education Act – and it needed to annex the surrounding land to expand the school quarters. When the unionists discovered that the prospective buyer of the land was a dummy bidder for the Bishop of Derry, they decided against selling the land to him. (St. Columb's was a junior seminary so the connection with the bishop was evident.)

In 1951, the St. Patrick's Day parade in Derry was baton-charged by the RUC in the city centre when the tricolour was raised by leading nationalist Eddie McAteer. The date has been etched in Derry's history as a terrible symbol of the status of Catholics at that time. Few journals ran with the story or published photographs of the disgraceful tactics deployed. However, an awareness of Northern Irish Catholics' plight was growing. The civil rights movement had not yet formed but already the Irish in England had begun to rally for reform in the North. Such incidents as the baton-charging of a St. Patrick's parade in Derry did not provoke much response; but it would be untrue to say that they caused no response. The support of the Irish in England during the 1950s inspired the civil rights movement in the North during the 1960s. As Anthony Coughlan put it:

'The abuses of the unionist state – the property franchise, gerrymandering and so on ... The marches staged by the Irish in England in the 1950s and early 1960s – one twelve day epic march from Liverpool to London – were forerunners of civil rights marches in the North itself (where protagonists stood to get batoned rather than ignored). Greater freedom existed in England at the time for such events. They were pivotal not only because they initiated the civil rights movement, but because they showed *the widely educated generation in the North that was about to come of age a mould in which they could agitate* [italics mine]. It was surely encouraging that feelings which were inchoate in the North were freely expressed in England. The Irish in England, just as Catholics in the North, realised that their interests were best served by aligning themselves with Labour' (Anthony Coughlan, *IRIS Magazine*, November 1988).

The civil rights movement gathered strength from such quarters when eventually it formed and took to the streets in Derry on 5 October 1968.

Even into the 1950s and 1960s, dockyard, shipyard and construction work was the pay-off to the Protestant working class. That labour was designated for them and kept beyond a lot of Catholics who didn't have enough work. So a sense that they were superior sustained working class Protestants. By the end of the 1960s, however, when a mass of Catholics were educated, the delicate foundation of the Protestant hegemony began to crack. The domination of Orange ideology, with its countless annual marches in July/August and its deftly organised pyramidal structure, had been usurped by emergent forces. There was the internal force of the 1947 generation. By 1968, influences external even to 'these islands' were exerting themselves: Prague protested the arrival of Soviet troops; Blacks in the southern states of America were determined to overcome their degraded status. Influences too strong to be penned in by drums and sashes had seeped into Ulster and the social revolution had begun. Deane called it 'the revelation'.

The Eleven Plus engendered an aspiration to enter the professions that had been up to that point all but completely absent among Catholics. Unionists feared that Derry – through Magee College or a new university – would have developed its own momentum. In 1966, Derry's unionists colluded in locating Ulster's second university in the east side of the province (where Protestantism is stronger), even though it meant doing down their own town. This angered Derry people immensely. While the civil rights movement had some negative consequences, things could not have remained as they were. By then the genie was out of the lamp.

The campaigners also brought, as Daly puts it in his interview, a 'new political language' to the debate and tossed out the old language of politics as a set of biased assumptions. As Deane wrote: 'Political languages fade more slowly than literary languages but when they do, they herald a deep structural alteration in the attitudes which sustain a crisis' (*Civilians and Barbarians*, 1983, p. 14, Field Day pamphlet).

A fundamental moment in which the history of Derry and Northern Ireland crystallised was 5 October 1968. It was a truly iconic day in the history of Northern Ireland. Basic reform of housing allocation and the electoral system were the goals of civil rights demonstrators. Northern Catholics may have been beaten off their streets on 5 October 1968 in the seminal march, partly organised by McCann – worse was to follow over the years – but it was not, fundamentally, a defeat. They were militarily repressed but politically vindicated in the eyes of the world. The echo went out. This day marked the beginning of many people's involvement with the civil rights movement. This day's importance in the history of the North simply cannot be overstated because it marked one of the glimpses of the power of the 1947 Education Act and the end of unionist Ulster as it had been constructed.

Reports in the media at the time record:

'Students from Queen's University Belfast hold a 3½ hour sit-down protest against police brutality in Derry on October 5th during civil rights march. After their protest, a delegation was allowed to see members of the Cabinet. They presented them with the following demands: one man, one vote, repeal of the Special Powers Act, the Public Order Act and the Flags and Emblems Act, the introduction of a Parliamentary Commissioner, a Human Rights Bill to be made law, the introduction of a points system for housing allocation, electoral boundaries to be re-drawn fairly, an impartial inquiry into police brutality in Derry on October 5th, and jobs to be allocated on the basis of ability' (CAIN Web Service, 9 October 1968).

The Free Derry Museum puts it well:

'Technology made the difference – the catalyst to expose misdeeds in Ulster. Pictures of RUC brutality were flashed around the world but the real impact was made by the footage recorded by an enterprising RTE cameraman [Gay O'Brien], who vividly recorded the panic and fear that the actions of the RUC provoked in Derry.'

Many things were in the air during the late sixties: the Beatles, the Rolling Stones, TV, Black American Liberation, the Soviet invasion of Prague. TV was crucial in spreading awareness to Derry Catholics of how their deprivation related to those other groups. It helped to show that the plight of Derry Catholics was similar to that of many other oppressed groups in the world. If James Baldwin, for example, were to have lived in Derry, he would have been an educated thorn in the side of the unionist state. Debating with a white man on TV during the American civil rights movement, James Baldwin argued:

> 'I don't know what most white people in this country feel, but I can only conclude what they feel from their institutions ... I don't know if the labour unions and union bosses really hate me. That doesn't matter. But I know I'm not in their unions. I don't know if the real estate lobbies are against black people, but I do know that they keep me in the ghetto. I don't know if the board of education hates black people, but I know its textbooks and its schools. Now this is the evidence. You want me to make an act of faith – risking my life, my woman, my sisters, my children – based on some idealism which you assure me exists in America which I have never seen.'

The emphasis on institutional discrimination is telling and one which was shared by the student protesters in Northern Ireland.

Protestant captains of industry saw no contradiction at this time in having as many as twenty-five votes. They had supplied jobs, hadn't they? They also believed themselves to be historically justified in possessing such power. Much of unionist history-writing down the ages has been nothing more than a legitimation for the containment of the native and the maintenance of a self-serving social structure. The following excerpt, taken from a Derry Protestant man's testimony in response to the incursions Catholics were beginning to make on the city in the late 1960s, reveals the 'siege mentality' in essence:

> 'We felt purely isolated and the Protestants in this city, where we'd been used all along, been told all along that it was the Protestant population that dominated the area, and then all of a sudden the whole thing was taken away from us – [we felt] total shock and unbelief at what was happening. It was like a drowning man that

was in the water and couldn't swim and couldn't do anything. Panic and fear set in' (Alistair Simpson, Fountain Resident, from Vinny Cunningham's *No Go – The Free Derry Story*, 2006.)

By whom had the Protestants been used all along if not the figures in the portraits painted on their own walls? They are still enshrined in the Fountainside: Queen Elizabeth II is an emblem of the monarchy that stretches back to the monarch who planted Ulster 400 years earlier. Protestant Ulster men had been used at the Somme. But the community continued to dominate the towns. Gratuitous plaques and statues were part of the pay-off. The triumphalism of Orange marches and bunting displays of Protestants in the North stands in contrast to their sedate Protestant counterparts in the Republic of Ireland today. The drawing of the border meant that All-Ireland Protestantism has never taken root as it should have done.

When Bogsiders cordoned off their territory in 1969 and declared it a 'No Go Area', unionists were made to realise that their territory was not guaranteed for the first time since partition. And territory was, after all, the purpose of their being in Ulster, a feudal precedent so hardwired to their identity that to lose – even the 888 acres of the Bogside, as the Bogside was then being defined – was tantamount to losing a part of themselves, their raison d'être. Their entire history was, in a sense, repudiated and retrospectively poisoned by this relatively minor advance from the Catholics. That is why the revolt of the Catholics was so painful. It is unsurprising that fear and panic were the animating principles of a people who had had their heritage brushed aside so thoughtlessly by the mother country. It is hard to avoid the conclusion that they had also been used by London from the very beginning. Token privileges (like calling Derry Londonderry) could hardly have sweetened the ultimate betrayal.

Why had they ceased to be useful? As McCann wrote:

'In the aftermath of October 5th [1968] the central thrust of British government policy was directed towards the "democratisation" of Northern Ireland. The increasing British investment in the Republic, the growing importance of the South of Ireland as a trading partner, made dangerously obsolete the traditional attitude of previous governments – one of un-critical support for the Unionist party in the North. For the first time in the history of Anglo-Irish relations it suited the Imperial power to balance between the Orange and the Green. This was automatically reflected in British policy towards the North. It involved a resolution to force concessions to the Catholics' (*The British Press and Northern Ireland*, 1972).

This perestroika dovetailed with the coming-of-age of the first post-1947 generation, the 'Eleven Plus Generation', and it constituted the biggest threat to unionist domination in the North in living memory. It was the first indication that the rug would be pulled imperceptibly from under the unionists' feet. Their response was visceral, harkening back centuries to their arrival in the North.

Gregory Campbell MP, reviewing the causes of the explosion in the North (*No Go – The Free Derry Story*), claimed that once the government talks to those who deny that that same government's writ runs in the Bogside, for example, then the seeds of insurrection are sown; the will to gain more independence and the will to overthrow the state grows. It should be emphasised that the British government, through its army, entered those negotiations in 1969 with Bogsiders over the head of Stormont, prefiguring direct rule from London three years later. What Campbell failed to note is that the overthrow of the government may be a desirable thing; that the status quo, which suited the people he represents as a politician, had severely handicapped Catholics in Derry for decades.

All this is not to say that British policy and nationalist sentiment overlapped serenely. Has it ever? A great deal of bitterness surfaced in the late 1960s and nationalists, having lived on the margins for so long, were not apt to trust the British authorities either. The British army had entered Derry on 14 August 1969. Initially, they were largely welcomed by many Bogsiders, who rightly saw this act as a wresting of power from the RUC whose cohort, the B-Specials, was soon to be disbanded. But the army soon grew hostile. The British army's casual attacks on Catholic citizens were – and remained for the next thirty years – the IRA's best recruiting tool. British soldiers were to stay in Derry until 1999/2000. The brutalities they visited upon Catholics is vividly recorded in McCann's *War and an Irish Town*. The RUC (later abetted by the British army) periodically engaged in Kristallnachts in the Bogside. This was surely what Phil Coulter intended when he wrote, 'With their tanks and the bombs/Oh my God, what have *they* done to the town I loved so well?' [Italics mine]. The RUC had no tanks and neither did the IRA. Coulter was referring to the supplementary military force of the British army in the late 1960s.

The environment in which the post-1947 generation grew up was repressive: RUC intimidation, suppression of St. Patrick's Day parades, the threat of internment without trial. The notion of agitating to achieve a democratic state was inchoate, but it was to be a few years before action could happen towards its realisation. As McCann put it: 'The interest of big businesses required the democratisation of the state – i.e. that the Specials be disbanded, the police disarmed, discrimination eliminated. It was not in its interest that, to take a random example, the state be overthrown' (*The British Press and Northern Ireland*). Here things did not, from the nationalist point of view, sit at all easily. Part of the reason for the escalation of violence in the North over these years was that the momentum nationalism got due to concessions inspired them to push for more. In the wake of a broken state (broken in the sense that the subordination of the minority as a fundamental aspect of its raison d'être was ended forever), a vacuum had been created that rival hardliners competed to fill.

The welfare state was the beginning of the end of the unionist state because it was forced to make the transition from a feudal to a modern capitalist society. All the violence in the North notwithstanding, slow and careful efforts to defuse what had passed were afoot. Eventually, with the foundation of Hume's party, the SDLP, the historic all-party discussions began at Sunningdale in 1973 – and the agreement was signed in December. Dublin reached an accord with London after the Sunningdale talks. Supporters of Paisley played a pivotal role in orchestrating the strike which subverted the Sunningdale Agreement. Paisley also campaigned to oust Brian Faulkner who had accepted the Council of Ireland, just as he had targeted Terence O'Neill who had, in 1969, accepted the concession of 'one man, one vote'.

Profiles of the Participants

Bishop Edward Daly

Bishop Daly was born in Belleek, Co. Fermanagh, in 1933. He boarded at St. Columb's in Derry City during the post-war period. After training in Rome as a priest, he returned to Ireland where he was curate in the Bogside and later became Bishop of Derry. An honorary Derry man, 'Eddie Daly' is very much a man of the people. All his life, he rallied for civil rights, justice for the wrongfully imprisoned and wrongfully accused.

John Hume

Hume was born in working class Derry in 1937, which had the worst housing in Europe at the time. In 1948, he passed the first year of the Eleven Plus exam. After studying in Maynooth, he returned to teach at St. Columb's. If he were to have been born in a different time, he may well have continued to teach at his alma mater but the conflict in Northern Ireland led him towards politics. His famous mantra was 'we'll spill our sweat, not our blood'.

He remained a remarkable parliamentarian during the most volatile years in the history of Northern Ireland. His prowess as a public speaker and as a negotiator, in addition to his charm and humility, were widely praised. The US President, Bill Clinton, worked closely with him during the peace process. His winning the Nobel Prize for Peace in 1998, with unionist leader David Trimble, symbolised progress in what once seemed an intractable situation.

Hume has given a lifetime to restoring peace to the North. His goals have always been egalitarian and respectful of both sides of the political divide.

John Hume, whose roots are in part Scottish Presbyterian, understood from a very early age that economics was a major force in transforming nations and bringing people together. In his Nobel Prize lecture, he spoke of having drawn inspiration from the way France and Germany had reconciled after WWII. He came to this realisation when he was in Strasbourg (a city to which Ambassador James Sharkey was later to be posted), a city that has reached a bi-cultural identity after the difficult birth of Franco-Germanic relations in the twentieth century.

Seamus Heaney

Heaney was born and raised on a small farm in south County Derry. He rose quickly in the university system, teaching in Queen's during his twenties. He has lectured in Harvard and held the prestigious Professor of Poetry chair for five years at Oxford. His poetry is world famous and has been cited by many as illuminating a way for the future. His works are translated into many languages. In 1995 he was awarded the Nobel Prize for Literature.

Seamus Deane

Deane was born in the Bogside. He became a specialist in the European Enlightenment while at Cambridge. He was general editor of James Joyce's work for Penguin and also editor of the *Field Day Anthology*. His scholarly insight has gained him international recognition. He is author of dozens of books and pamphlets. He held the chair of Irish Literature at Notre Dame University, Indiana. He has also published four books of poetry. A novel he wrote about his childhood, *Reading in the Dark*, was shortlisted for the Booker Prize in 1996. Like Eamonn McCann, another major left-wing thinker in Ireland today, Seamus Deane lends enormously to the international aspect of this generation.

Eamonn McCann

McCann is another from the Bogside who has proved himself as a writer and social thinker. He helped to mastermind the October 5th civil rights march and 'Battle of the Bogside' which resulted in 'The Free Derry Movement' – events that held the world in awe during the late sixties. He was eye-witness to many of the atrocities committed by the British army and thus he became an invaluable reporter on the Saville Trial – an inquiry into Bloody Sunday. He is author of dozens of books and pamphlets about this and related matters. A renowned newspaper columnist, he regularly features on BBC and Irish TV programmes. McCann has said that he 'never had a patriotic sentiment in his life'. His motivations have always been for equality for everyone on the socialist model.

Phil Coulter

Coulter is from Derry City, off Bishop Street, quite near St. Columb's. His father was an officer in the Royal Ulster Constabulary. He evinced great talent for music early on. While still at Queen's University, his songwriting potential began to attract attention. His first major breakthrough came in 1967 when his song, 'Puppet on a String', won the Eurovision contest. He also wrote 'Congratulations', a song that finished second in the same competition the following year. He wrote 'My Boy' for Elvis Presley. He has collaborated with Planxty, Tom Jones, Van Morrison and the Rolling Stones. He has won some 23 platinum records, 39 gold and 52 silver albums.

Phil Coulter's song lyrics have extolled 'tomorrow and peace once again'. These sentiments surely harken to his background and his father's occupation – an RUC officer.

Ambassador James Sharkey

Born of this generation in the Bogside, James Sharkey entered the Foreign Service at the age of 26. At the age of 44, he became one of the youngest Ambassadors in the history of Ireland. His posts have included Australia, Scandinavia, Russia, America, Italy, the United States, Japan and Switzerland.

Everywhere he has gone, he has left evidence of his illustrious career behind. St. Patrick's Day parades on the main streets of Oslo and Tokyo were his initiatives. He has also published on topics of the many cultures he has visited. He has lived all over the globe and speaks several languages. Tip O'Neill has written on his achievement.

Paul Brady

Brady comes from Strabane, County Tyrone. Even as a teenager, he began to make his name in Ireland as a singer. An album he released with Andy Irvine of Planxty (1976) catapulted him to international stardom. He has since sold out world tours; some of his albums have remained in the Irish charts for 30 weeks. He is a prolific songwriter. His best known song is, arguably, 'Paradise is Here' sung by Tina Turner.

The Boys of St. Columb's

Father Anthony C. McFeely (President of St. Columb's, 1951–59) got the nickname Sam. He was also known as 'The Dome' because of his hairless head. One past student described him as being 'tough but fair', the priest without hair. Boys used to say:

'I see The Dome.
The Dome sees me –
Way up in the gallery.
Please let the light
That shines on me
Shine on The Dome
In the gallery.'

It seems fitting to open the section of this book which reproduces the testimonies of eight 'Boys of St. Columb's' with a panoptic image. The school and the church meshed in one institution and seldom took their eyes off potential priests and the future leaders of Ireland. There were Big Brother forces in the school and fearsome punishments to enforce the ethos of the place. 'It was of its time ...' the received wisdom goes. And it was. But there is more to it. St. Columb's was also a peculiarly placed school – geographically and politically – and one that underwent an enormous transition very quickly. These shifts are embodied in the testimonies of its students.

Edward Daly

St. Columb's boarders were often bigger than day-boys, partly because a lot of them had been raised on farms where food was plentiful, if not gourmet. Few of the socioeconomic reasons for privations meant much to an eleven year old up from the farm. Indeed, it came as quite a shock – added to the shock of beginning to board – that they would not have enough food to eat; and no prospect of remedying that condition until Christmas. Boarders who happened to come from the Republic of Ireland were on average two years senior to their Derry City day-boy counterparts, starting grammar school at thirteen years of age. Mothers of prospective boarders believed that boarding would give boys regularity. In the case of farmers' sons, they would be kept at study rather than at work on the farm on evenings. On the boarder/day-boy distinction, Bishop Daly wrote, 'We considered ourselves superior to day-boys, of course, whilst, at the same time, being deeply envious of them' (*Seeking the Kingdom*, p. 62). The regime was tough. The evening schedule for boarders ran: 5.00– 5.55, study; 5.55–6.05, cigarette break (senior boarders had a smoking room); 6.05–7.30, study; 7.30–8.30, dinner; 8.30–10.00, study.

One member who attended St. Columb's during the post-war period remembers the school as a reasonably fair place:

> 'We had no notion of abstract theories of justice; you just took things as they were. Tom and Paddy Mullarky and Seamus Heaney were a year behind me. There was a strong camaraderie among the boarders. In 1950, there was still rationing. The fee for boarding for Southerners was fifty pounds per annum.'

In 1947, there were approximately 300 boarders and 200 day-boys. Year by year, conditions at the school ameliorated slightly. Full and partial scholarships became available after 1947. Full scholarship covered both boarding fees and tuition. Boys from Northern Ireland did not have to pay tuition; boys from the Republic did. That boarding school during this era was tough is indubitable. One luxury that boarders in St. Columb's did have was that they could walk. 'The Walks', as they were known, were designated for meditative exercise.

Rules were absolute in St. Columb's. In the 1950s, when the circus came to Derry, a group of boarders sneaked out to attend. When they were spotted, their truancy became an international incident. There was a tremendous brouhaha and they were expelled. Although their parents tried to intercede, the Dean's decision was final. That was the standard attitude at the time. (This was an era when birching and hanging people were accepted.) It is important to remember that their generation inherited this hard regime; it did not invent it. Secondary education had been inaccessible up to that point and college staff felt that they could exercise severe discipline on students. Soft and generous Derry people did not make boarders feel like outsiders, and the Derry decency was there too: when brutality happened, Derry people hopped in on behalf of others. Young and lay teachers relied less on corporal punishment.

Day-boys bought cigarettes in Johnny's Shop after school. Day-boys came predominantly from Derry City, so there was a factional element to the day-boy/boarder distinction. Outside the school, when they saw a member of the clergy or a teacher on the street, they gave a military salute, even outside school hours. (The teachers, even the severe ones, would reciprocate.)

Added to the severity of boarding circumstances, the preferred method of educating was quite violent. I spoke to a St. Columb's boy who, at the age of 66, still has nightmares that an Irish exam is coming up and about his Irish teacher's brutality. Similarly, when he drives into Derry City and sees Craigavon Bridge, his heart partially sinks and the dread of St. Columb's steals over him. Senior Prefects gathered in 'The Libs' (The Library) on Saturday to dish out punishments on carefully selected boys.

Boarders were 'culchies'. (The word culchie derives from Kiltimagh, a small town in Co. Mayo, and it denotes someone who is irredeemably rustic.) Boarders were quite a new presence for Derry City boys who are to this day socially promiscuous, good mixers. Day-boys were not in the habit of traveling beyond Craigavon Bridge. The boys from the Republic had a grounding in the Irish language. They had to adapt to the ways of St. Columb's rather than vice versa. The Irish national ethos didn't impinge on the curriculum as it was determined by the Northern Irish Government.

There were small modifications even between Bishop Daly's time as a boarder and Heaney's entry into St. Columb's a few years later. For example, by that time St. Columb's boys got three days free at Halloween. The first time boarders got out of St. Columb's on a regular basis was when the swimming pool was founded in Derry.

After a period in Rome, Daly returned to the North and found himself located in the Bogside as a curate in 1962. This was a Derry he had never experienced before. The Bogside that Daly encountered was, as he says in the interview, a revelation to the young curate. Families were enormous. Fifteen children in a family was not uncommon. One O'Doherty family had twenty-one children – in a 'two up, two down' house with an outdoor toilet. Derry was also brimming with stories. The Celtic Chippy was mythologised in the area. The owner, Brennan, did a very tasty (what to this day is known in Derry as) 'Fish Supper'. People came from miles around to buy his fish and chips. He took his much sought after recipe for batter with him to the grave.

There was a great deal of variation in the Bogside. People from certain streets that are now classified as being in the Bogside would have taken umbrage in the 1950s and 1960s to hear them referred to as such. Respectable families had high standards in everything – education, social conduct and observation of the faith. Middle class people from the Bogside moved out as soon as the Troubles started. Before the Eleven Plus, fees deterred the working class from going to school. Even post-1947, persuading the working class to go to school remained a problem. In this interview, Daly also elaborates on the importance of the arrival of television to the Bogside. The McDaids got the first TV on a certain street in the Bogside; they opened the window and people watched it from the street.

The Bogside was and is very much an open-door community. At the time of a birth, all the women would gravitate towards the house of the woman in labour. Men skedaddled. Midwives usually arrived in time, but many ordinary women were quite capable of delivering a child. All babies of this generation were delivered at home. When hospital delivery became de rigueur, only over the Matron's dead body were relatives allowed inside the hospital.

Football went hand and hand with Bogside culture. One footballer who came from the Bogside reflected on the Northern Irish divide:

> 'Even though my community was ultra nationalist, there was no problem in returning back from playing football in Coleraine (a largely Protestant town). In Coleraine I was exposed to a culture in my teens that my peers still have not encountered. I made friendships that survived to this day.'

He also remembers that Sir Basil McFarrell, a unionist in the town, once requested a well-known singer to sing for him. In return, the singer's family had a house in no time – and ahead of a footballer's family. But the singer's family looked after their own. They put the footballer's family up until they also were allotted a house.

The divide between GAA and soccer in St. Columb's was stark. The College was resolute on the sporting ethos it wanted to sponsor: GAA, an all-Ireland sport, was lauded and soccer was scorned. During this time boarders such as Daly were not allowed to play soccer at St. Columb's.

The GAA ban on 'foreign games' seems to have been, especially in the North, a mirror image of the unionist-orientated media in Belfast. In the interview, Bishop Daly speaks of GAA sports not being broadcast on the BBC during his youth. The intensity of the intolerance of the one induced the intolerance of the other.

MF: Can you speak a little about your background, where you grew up?

ED: The family home was just outside the village of Belleek in County Fermanagh, about a hundred yards from the border between what is now called the Republic of Ireland and Northern Ireland. The River Erne, then and now, marked the border between County Fermanagh and County Donegal. It was a wonderful place to grow up – a little isolated, perhaps. There were lots of things to do – football, fishing, rabbit hunting, reading and helping on the farm and in the shop. There was very good radio reception of Radio Éireann and poor reception from the BBC. There was a much visited cinema in Ballyshannon nearby. I learned music with my mother. Then World War II began – children, evacuees began to arrive from Belfast, England and Scotland. The RAF established a very big air base between Belleek and Enniskillen, and also a sea plane base on Lough Erne which was a fascinating thing for a youngster. Dozens and dozens of seaplanes, the Sunderlands and Catalinas, as well as land-based aircraft were going overhead all of the time. We were right under de Valera's so-called 'Donegal Corridor', although we were not to know that for many years afterwards. Thousands of American GIs were based between Belleek and Enniskillen and prepared there for the campaign in Europe. Tanks and all the paraphernalia of war and battle were common sights. It was a very exciting and stimulating childhood for a young boy.

Then the time came to go to second level school. I sat an entrance examination and was sent to St. Columb's College.

MF: So you came to St. Columb's in 1946. How would you assess the education you received there?

ED: The education was good, certainly. Some of the teachers were excellent. One learned a lot about academic subjects, a lot of French, a lot of Latin, mathematics and a lot of English. But at the same time we learned very little about life.

MF: What change did 1947 bring to St. Columb's?

ED: After the 1947 Education Act, the numbers of day pupils and boarders increased quite dramatically. Afterwards I became keenly conscious of the impact it had on the social and political life of the North. But at a time of harsh post-war rationing, my primary social concern was avoiding hunger, wondering about the next parcel from home, and when the holidays would be – and avoiding harsh punishments. One of the things that you really learned at St. Columb's, as a boarder, was survival. A lot of the pupils would have been lucky enough to have relatives in Derry they could have visited; I didn't have any and it was a very lonely time – being cold, lonely and hungry are my abiding memories – not the happiest years of my life. It is very hard to envisage the situation now as it was then. But it was difficult and you certainly grew up very quickly.

MF: Can you speak about your early life as a priest?

ED: After I was ordained in 1957, I was appointed to Castlederg in County Tyrone, which was an interesting place. It was the first time in my life that I experienced the rawness of the political and sectarian divide in Northern Ireland because that town was very much split between the two. There were a lot of tensions in the area at that time, the legacy of an election campaign just before I arrived. There were still some of the sensitivities that lingered on. They were very formative years. The local people were delightful and I learned much from them. During my years there political tensions eased. I had a lot of contact with Protestant people. I got involved with shows and running concerts and plays – the dramatic society, that sort of thing. That is a great way of communicating with people. It is a great way of getting to work with people and also establishing friendships of various kinds.

MF: When did you come back to Derry?

ED: In May 1962, I was appointed as curate in St. Eugene's Cathedral. I was there until June 1973, during what proved to be a very dramatic period.

A thing I remember about Derry was the humour of the place. The wit was extraordinary. It was really a pleasure to go around houses talking to people, getting to know them and allowing them to get to know me.

The district I was given at that time was the Bogside. Now the Bogside at that time was a relatively small area. It has expanded enormously since then in people's minds, but at that time, it was quite a small compact area. It consisted of Wellington Street, Nelson Street, the Bogside, Carlisle Place, Rossville Street, Fahan Street, Joseph Street, Foxes Corner, Pilot's Row, Eden Place, Adam's Close, Chamberlain Street, High Street and Harvey Street, Abbey Street, Frederick Street, Union Street, Thomas Street and Anne Street. There were a huge number of people living there. There was overcrowding that was quite unimaginable. I never thought that people in Ireland lived in such conditions that they lived in – twenty people living in a four-roomed house. Unbelievable conditions. The one thing I remember about the Bogside is that houses were full of beds – upstairs rooms, downstairs rooms were all full of beds. People lived, reared families, cooked, washed and slept in the one room. How they did it, I don't know. There was a tap in the back yard, no running water inside. They boiled whatever water they wanted to heat – to wash nappies, to cook, to wash themselves. There was an outside toilet. And people, women particularly, were remarkable. I was enormously impressed by the women and their caring mentality and their good humour, their love for their children. They also were the breadwinners. They worked in the factories. The worst single conditions I experienced were at a place over in East Wall, which was around the City Walls, just off Foyle Street. There was a building there that I will never forget. There must have been twenty families living in it, shocking conditions. It was a huge tenement house. The smell was absolutely revolting.

It was not an accident that people were living in these situations. This was brought about for political reasons. People were forced to live in those situations to facilitate the continuing power and authority of one particular group in the city. I visited every family in the Bogside, in my district, at least once every year and in some cases on many occasions each year. They were wonderful people.

MF: Can you speak a little more about the political reasons for the Bogside? What changed it eventually?

ED: Those places had been gerrymandered to ensure that that minority would maintain control of the local government, the city council. John Hume got together with Paddy 'Bogside' Doherty and some others in the city and set up the Credit Union, which liberated people from moneylenders, which was one of the plagues of the society. Subsequently they formed the Derry Housing Association, which again broke the control that unionists had over housing. It was in the early '60s, in the middle 1960s, that that suddenly impacted on everything here. When the first products of the 1947 Education Act emerged from universities here – Eamonn McCann, John Hume and quite a number of others – they could articulate the grievances of the people from the area in a way that could be understood by those living there and by the media. Television came to Derry in the 1960s. People had televisions and that was literally a window on the world for people here.

They realised that people around the world didn't live in situations like they experienced; that this was an aberration, not normal. People like John Hume, Eamonn McCann and others articulated those grievances which people immediately identified with. They protested about it and gradually that air of protest, of facing up to this huge political authority strengthened. They got off their knees. In the 1960s, Martin

Luther King's civil rights movement demonstrated that there could be revolution or protest without violence, because this, I think, inhibited people before that: that if you started protesting there would be violence, the same as there was in the 1920s [Irish Civil War, 1922-23]. People who had just emerged from university, highly intelligent, highly articulate natives of the Bogside, provided the leadership. They started to speak a whole new political language and that evoked a response from within people.

MF: How did this new generation of educated Catholics bring about liberation?

ED: To my mind education is liberation. People who are educated, able to think, able to articulate their grievances, are liberated by that. Locally, the *Derry Journal* was the paper and the *Londonderry Sentinel*, but they were very conservative. They didn't rock the boat too much. There wasn't a television outlet here in the city. Everything was centred on Belfast and everything in Belfast was unionist-oriented. The breakthrough that was made into the media was very, very important because for the first time the voice of the people was heard. The real breakthrough was the march of 5 October 1968. I was enraged when I heard what had happened there. And there was rioting here that night – the first time we ever had rioting in Derry was that Saturday night. People got off their knees and said, 'we're not going to have any more of this. We want equal citizenship'. They attacked the business vote and all the structures of the gerrymander that we had here. That was attacked root and branch at that time.

I took part in all the marches in the late '68 period except for the first one. And I can say they were subjected to violence rather than being initiators of it. Admittedly, they were marching in places that were said to be illegal by people like William Craig at that time. But they were marching in their own city.

And I'm embarrassed even now that I didn't rise up against it before then. We were very much still touching the forelock in the 1960s. It took people like Eamonn McCann, John Hume and other people to come along and shake us out of our complacency. As Eamonn would have said, to get us off our knees.

MF: What would you say to the criticism – voiced by Conor Cruise O'Brien – that nonviolent protest elicits violence?

ED: It's very difficult to say. I mean, what do you do? Do you do nothing? Just sit back and watch people live in those situations and suffer the injustice and indignities that they suffered? These people were a little reluctant to raise their voices because they were afraid of starting off another situation like the one between 1916 and 1921 – the rioting and the subsequent civil war. But at the same time, this thing was just too profound and too unjust to allow it to be ignored.

But there is a danger in any situation where you do protest and there is a very firm resistance by the forces of government. That's the irresistible force meeting the immovable object. And something's going to give. And in incidents like that, hotter heads do prevail. And that's what happened here. Despite the fact that the civil rights movement achieved almost all of their aims in Derry – about housing, about voting, about the local corporation that was prorogued (that was the city council) – still it tumbled over into violence. The pent-up frustration of generations suddenly burst forth. The depth of hurt was so great and also, gradually, the intense dislike of the RUC – from accepting them with a grudging respect – suddenly grew to a huge hostility. We tumbled into the vortex I suppose.

MF: Can you remember one of the earliest incidents of the Troubles, involving Sammy Devenney?

ED: He was given a dreadful beating in his own home – I knew Sammy for many years. He worked for a local undertaker – he was a quiet, inoffensive man. I remember, I was in the house, just fifteen minutes afterwards. He was in a dreadful condition, beaten black and blue. Such cruelty – a totally innocent man. It was just awful.

MF: Phil Coulter's 'The Town I Loved So Well' depicts Derry of that time. What are your feelings about that song?

ED: I think Phil Coulter's song 'The Town I Loved So Well' encapsulates the atmosphere of the mid-1970s in Derry very well, catching that atmosphere in a remarkable, uncanny way. I think Luke Kelly singing it always adds another dimension to that song; he gives expression to the anger.

I can identify enormously with what Phil was getting at. I have known Phil since he was a teenager in the 1960s – I used to go to parties at his house – and they were great parties.

MF: How do you view your boarding school education now?

ED: I envy young people today who live at home, go to second level school, study at home, and have a social life during their teenage years and so forth. We didn't experience that in our growing up in Fermanagh … I wish we had. But there was no option in my time – if you wanted a second level education, you had to leave home. If I lived life again and if I had a son or daughter, I would never send them to boarding school. I think it deprives them of so much.

MF: Why do you think so many fine minds emerged from St. Columb's at this time?

ED: First and foremost, there were some superb teachers. Besides, I think it may have been the mixture of people from a rural background mixing on a day to day basis, in class all day every day, with people from an urban background – the kind of chemistry that took place in St. Columb's in the early and mid-50s especially. I think you had the coming together of two different cultures. This was the first group of people who had the experience of getting from education everything that education had to offer, thanks to the 1947 Education Act. They got educated to the fullness of their capacity – to go to second level school, to go to university subsequently, to achieve the fullness of their potential. They were the first group of people from their community and their families who had that experience. The experience of living in a situation like the Bogside itself was a very powerful education, but that combined with academic education, with kids who came from different backgrounds in the country. Perhaps that created the chemistry that produced this synthesis.

MF: You continued to live administering the faith, in your adopted town?

ED: I must say I've been blessed to have lived through those times. It was a remarkable experience. In the latter years, from '71 onwards, when the conflict looked very bad and when they started using CS gas extensively, I made it my business to be in the Bogside, Rossville Street particularly, to help in the evacuation of older people.

MF: Would you speak about your recollections of January 30th, 1972, Bloody Sunday?

ED: I have told the story, in detail, countless times. On that day, heavily armed British paratroopers, professional soldiers, murdered thirteen innocent, unarmed people and seriously injured many others in a period of less than twenty minutes. This dreadful crime was perpetrated in full view of hundreds of people, including journalists, television and radio reporters and cameramen. One of their commanding officers was decorated. Nobody was ever charged with any offence. That, briefly, is the story of that afternoon.

John Hume

John Hume comes bustling into the lobby of a Derry hotel a few minutes late. Hand in his pocket, he is already greeting old acquaintances with 'who am I talking to?' I order the drinks and point to a free table. He remains standing, but when two ladies hover near the seat he says assertively, 'that seat is taken'. They laugh and seem honoured to have been spoken to – if only in rebuke – by a Nobelist. He enjoys the encounter too.

Hume is shrunken from the big man he was when standing on the Nobel podium in Oslo in 1998. He is still able to launch into an address of how the situation in the North changed as a result of the Education Act of 1947: 'The great wealth of the world is people. The measure of economies is how they are used. I went to Rosemount primary school and we were prepared well for the Eleven Plus. They had to build huts in St. Columb's to accommodate the influx of students after 1947.'

As Hume put it, 'What changed the situation eventually – and, of course, it took a lot of time to change it, things like that don't change in a week or a fortnight – was the new educational system' (*Seeking the Kingdom*).

After earning his MA at Maynooth, Hume was ready for a job in St. Columb's. Hume taught History and French at St. Columb's from 1960 to 1967. He used to invite Paddy Gormley of the Nationalist Party to speak to classes at St. Columb's. Aside from nationalism, Hume used to teach boys about the Credit Union, informing rather than proselytising.

In any scale of values which ranks community work highly, Hume is exemplary. It was concern for the development of his community that drew him away from his steady teaching job. Another young teacher at St. Columb's, Cathal Logue, who taught with Hume, remembers talking to Hume at a radiator between classes. Hume was convinced that the political scene could be changed and he was considering doing something to effect that change.

Entering the political scene at a time when politics is opening up gives an unusual importance to the personality of the leader. Unlike other interviewees in this book, Hume was not part of the Wolfe Tone Club whose meetings took place at Glenbrook Terrace. His father would tell him that 'you cannot eat a flag', and thus Hume's politics were imbued with a strong strain of pragmatism from his early youth which helped him to reconcile the seemingly irreconcilable. Nationalist mythology of blood-sacrifice jarred with Hume's exhortation of the efficacy of peaceful means and a sworn stance against violence.

Gerrymandering made Derry a deeply unjust place. Many unionists, however, did not think of the Guildhall in Derry as an unjust place. The system was entirely self-perpetuating. Many believed that Catholics did not have jobs because they were socially crippled by having big families and uninterested in work – rather than this being the consequence of the present political structure.

One of Hume's major legacies is the founding of the Credit Union in the Bogside. Up to that point, as Daly remembers, many Bogsiders had been at the mercy of loan sharks. Hume ended that culture and he rightly considers it one of his most important contributions to his city. The Bogside was ripe for independent credit institutions because the mould was already created for them by certain prominent citizens. For example, Hugh Mailey, a publican, was a Credit Union unto himself. He never allowed men to drink their wages. (Mailey's was one of the last bastions against women in pubs. Later it melted a bit – women were allowed to sit in snugs.) A principled man, he never let anyone overindulge on his premises. Men also drank in the Celtic Bar, especially on Friday nights. Eldest boys would arrive to the window on Fridays to collect their father's wages on behalf of their mothers. It was an honour-

able, decent place as well. The publican, John Bradley, made sure that wives got the bulk of their husband's wages.

It cannot be emphasised enough that protest was not the civil rights movement's first or preferred approach to politics. Many in the civil rights movement had also supported the Derry Housing Association, led by Hume, in the 1960s. When Hume succeeded in raising funds and gaining planning for new housing the city council, extending the gerrymander, stultified the plan. Feeling that they had no alternative, they hit the streets to protest the injustice.

Hume's initiatives in the locality of Derry suddenly took on international significance in 1968. A mass of disenchanted, dispossessed people were now on the street, protesting for civil rights. In 1968, Protestants started to flee their middle-class housing and Catholics rapidly took their place.

As Phil Coulter says in his interview, the default position of the Nationalist Party up to the 1960s had been that of anti-partition – walking out of meetings, opposing the political structure in place in Northern Ireland. The Social Democratic and Labour Party (SDLP), which Hume helped to found and went on to lead, was a reformulation of the Nationalist Party but it was profoundly different in its approach to constitutional nationalism. The SDLP was a modernisation of Eddie McAteer's Nationalist Party which had, by the late 1960s, gone out of fashion and did not have very inspiring leadership. History seemed to fall into place for Hume. Hume brought credibility to Constitutional Nationalism. Youth was the secret in those days. He was – which is very rare – an intelligent man who got roped into politics from his involvement with the Credit Union onwards. He led people who were the beneficiaries of free education: they took the authorities on non-violently and they could no longer be ignored. Hume's approach was the opposite of walking out. It was to sit-in. It was to insist that opposing sides come to the negotiating table. It was to answer the threat of physical force with unassailable rationale. A good example of Hume's resilience in the face of adversity came during the Sunningdale Agreement negotiations. Working night and day to induce five parties from England and Ireland, North and South, to agree on the Sunningdale Agreement in 1973/4, Hume and the SDLP had, to deepen anxieties, a provincial-wide unionist strike with which to contend. Unionism, in its extremist form, was bent on subverting the finest agreement that could be established in the North (one which was ratified, in essence, over twenty years of violence later on Good Friday, 1998). Hume had brought the deal on the table and was determined to push it through. Disproving McCann's hasty labelling of the SDLP as 'middle-aged, middle-class and middle-of-the-road', Hume was adamant that Sunningdale should succeed. When the water supply was cut in Derry and the sewage system failed as part of the unionist strike he said, 'I'll sit here until there is shit flowing up Royal Avenue and then the people will realise what these people are about and then we'll see who wins'. (*John Hume: A Biography*, by Paul Routledge, Harper Collins, 1997, p. 134). Deane saw in Harold Wilson's failure to stand up to the recalcitrance of unionists over Sunningdale 'a sinister indication that you could be rewarded for bigotry' (*Journal of Irish Studies*, Japan, Vol. 21). History will record it – though Sunningdale failed – as Hume's finest hour. And the best chance of justice in the North was squandered.

When Hume helped to found the SDLP in 1970, a party he led from 1979, social reform was at the heart of his concerns. In Derry the need for housing reform in particular was stark. The SDLP outshone and ultimately supplanted the Nationalist Party, not only because its new blood advocated an agenda that spoke to the newly educated population, but also because they revealed that social change took precedence over nationalism in the electorate's concerns.

(Social reform has trumped ideological leanings at the hustings for years. In the course of his decades of campaigning, the great Labour thinker and leader James Connolly also came to realise that, irrespective of the virtues of worldwide socialism, social reform within the Irish national framework was crucially needed by his followers. He was executed in a chair by the British Army in 1916 for his part in proclaiming Ireland an independent republic.)

Hume realised his people's priorities from the first. The SDLP gained such support in Derry and beyond because the party responded to many long awaited needs. In the following passage, Deane comments on Hume's consistent electoral success and its greater appeal than Eamonn McCann's socialist agenda:

> 'The reality for the PDs' [People's Democracy] situation is this. They are becoming increasingly out of touch, increasingly doctrinaire. Along with McCann they will starve for want of the popular support they are so expert at losing. John Hume could beat their combined forces in any given constituency in the North. His kind of ambitious moderation can be sneered at, of course, but only so long as McCann and the PDs restrict themselves to largely symbolic actions and regard their failure to reach power as a form of purity' ('Mugwumps and Reptiles', *Atlantis*, 1972, p. 10).

That success continued for the rest of Hume's career. Deane's comment would also have held true had Hume contested an all-Ireland election such as the Presidency. No statesman on the island of Ireland in the latter part of the twentieth century generated support to match Hume's once he had established himself. Hume was the man who pushed in the South 'ambitious moderation' on the Northern question. The latent support for Hume in the Republic only grew in proportion to the South's turning away from the IRA.

Past pupils of St. Columb's learned the art of negotiation which they took with them to Westminister, Washington or wherever they went. Hume in particular had about him an impatient clarity, especially when confronted with indifference to the plight of the people he represented. The following dialogue records Hume remonstrating with a British soldier on Magilligan Beach on 23 January 1972 (one week before Bloody Sunday).

Hume: Are you proud of the way your men have treated this crowd today?

Soldier: This crowd has tried to come into a prohibited area.

Hume: You shot them with rubber bullets ... The crowd was marching over there. The leaders were going to speak to you and before we even got here you opened fire ... I wouldn't be very proud of the conduct of your men today. They opened fire on a crowd of people and they were totally unarmed people.

Soldier: You are not allowed to march in there.

Hume: Why not?

Soldier: It is prohibited.

Hume: It does not belong to you. You cannot say ...

Soldier: It is directed by your government.

Hume: [shouts] Who's government?

Soldier: The government of Northern Ireland.

Hume: Not our government. And that's why you're here – because it is not our government.'

(The Stormont Government was prorogued by Westminster later that year.)

In January 1996, Bill Clinton – in Derry's Guildhall – said he was proud 'to be here in the home town of Ireland's most tireless champion for civil rights, and its most eloquent voice for non-violence, John Hume'. When Hume won his Nobel Prize, Seamus Heaney wrote the following:

> 'When I knew John Hume at St. Columb's College, Derry, in the 1950s, he already displayed the qualities that have led him to this new eminence. You had the impression of somebody reliable and consistent, who operated from a principled and definite mental centre' (*Irish Times*, 17 October 1998).

Having achieved so much in every arena he encountered, Hume's place in history is surely secure.

MF: What impact did the 1947 Education Act and its auxiliary exam, the Eleven Plus, have on your area?

JH: The introduction of the Eleven Plus transformed the area in many ways. It transformed this college, because before the Eleven Plus the only people who attended this college would have been the sons of business and professional people. It led also to the expansion of the college in terms of its buildings. I was very fortunate that I passed the Eleven Plus in its very first year.

MF: What impact did it have on you personally?

JH: I was very, very lucky that I wasn't a year older because I would have missed the Eleven Plus and I wouldn't have been educated. Education has transformed my life as it does to everybody else's life. And of course primary schools also made an enormous contribution. Education is one of the most important things in any country. It is no accident that what the poorest countries in the world, third world countries, all have in common is that they have no real education system. There's no doubt of the value of education. It should never be underestimated.

The fact that education, higher education, was available to all sections of the community, and particularly those from working class backgrounds, transformed the community.

MF: How did the education that your generation received change things in Derry?

JH: It was that generation that later founded the civil rights movement to improve this city and to end the enormous discrimination that existed. In those days, although only 30 per cent of the population was unionist, they governed the city by a system of gerrymander. The civil rights movement began to take on that and began to change that.

MF: Why did the civil rights movement come to particular prominence here in Derry?

JH: The civil rights movement was very strong here in the city of Derry because Derry was the worst example of the lack of civil rights in Northern Ireland, and indeed it was the worst example of the injustice of Northern Ireland. The voting system was created to ensure that unionists remained in charge. The city was divided into voting areas, and the largest voting area was where the vast majority of Catholics lived. Unionists lived in the other two areas. They won every election. Even though the large majority was Catholic, they didn't have as many seats.

MF: Is it fair to say that the 1947 Education Act led directly to the 1968 civil rights movement?

JH: Well, the 1968 civil rights movement was heavily inspired by the existence of the civil rights movement in the United States – Martin Luther King. It wouldn't have had the same support as it had, or leadership that it had, if it hadn't been for the transformation of the education system.

I did a thesis on the history of Derry in the early centuries when it was growing outside the walls – 'Derry Beyond the Walls' was my thesis. I got an MA degree for that.

MF: Yes, I read that thesis – very interesting. You wrote about how the drawing of the border strangulated Derry's economy. Could you elaborate on that point a little?

JH: When the border was drawn, Derry was very unfortunate because Derry's natural hinterland was Inishowen – Derry was the capital of Inishowen – and yet, with the drawing of the border, it lost all that. It's no accident that in the early days after the border was created, the

North-West was the poorest area in the whole of Ireland, and had the area of highest unemployment.

MF: How well did the education you received at St. Columb's equip you for life?

JH: I got a university scholarship and I ended up with a degree in French and History which was very well taught in St. Columb's College.

MF: To what extent did St. Columb's form you and prepare you?

JH: If it hadn't been for St. Columb's I couldn't have made the progress that I made in the world.

MF: Sean B. O'Kelly had a remarkable influence as an English teacher. Isn't that so?

JH: Mr O'Kelly was very well known as an English teacher and he was a great teacher of English. That was proved by the achievements of his pupils like Seamus Deane and Seamus Heaney.

MF: Your parents' generation did not have the chance of education?

JH: Our parents' generation certainly wasn't educated very much at all. My father was unemployed, although he was a very able man. During the war he was employed by the food office in Derry because he was a copperplate handwriter. All the ration books for the city were in his handwriting. People used to come to him very regularly. He used to write letters for them, advise them on approaches to problems that they had. I grew up in poverty. So from a very young age, I was very well aware of people's problems.

MF: Why did you resign from your teaching position here in St. Columb's?

JH: Well, I stopped being a teacher because I had an idea about doing something in relation to local development. I had been heavily involved in forming the Credit Union movement. The River Foyle was one of the biggest salmon rivers in the whole of Europe. Our salmon was exported to other countries to be smoked, and I used to argue that we should smoke our own salmon. And one of my friends, Michael Canavan, said, 'right, we'll start it up,' and I gave up my job.

MF: Can you speak a little about your relationship with the Irish in America?

JH: I made very strong contacts in the United States. I made contact with and became very friendly with Edward Kennedy, Tip O'Neill, who was speaker of the American Congress, Dan Moynihan and Hugh Carey – those four became known as the 'four horsemen' because they

gave very strong support for the achievement of civil rights in Northern Ireland.

MF: You always believed that the Northern conflict could be solved without violence?

JH: When the basis of a problem is a divided people, violence has no role to play in solving it. What violence then does is simply deepen the division. If you are campaigning for civil rights, for equality of treatment, how can you use methods which undermine the fundamental human right, the right to life?

MF: How did it feel to win the Nobel Prize?

JH: I was very honoured to win the Nobel Prize, and I saw that as a very strong international statement by the Nobel Prize people of support for peace in our streets.

MF: You spoke once about being in Strasbourg and the inspiration you drew from how the Germans and the French had reconciled their differences. Maybe you could speak a little about that?

JH: When I first went to Strasbourg in France as a member of the European Parliament, I went for a walk across the bridge from Strasbourg in France to Kehl in Germany. I stood in the middle of the bridge, and I meditated. I said, 'Good Lord, there's France, there's Germany'. If I had stood here at the end of the Second World War thirty years ago, and thought then, don't worry, it's all over, in thirty years you will all be together in a united Europe, I would have been sent to a psychiatrist. But that's exactly what happened. The European Union is the best example in the history of the world of conflict resolution, I thought. And therefore it should be studied. And when you look at the principles at the heart of the European Union, those are the principles that should be implemented in any area of conflict in the world. The three principles at the heart of the European Union are the same three principles at the heart of the Good Friday Agreement in Northern Ireland.

Principle number one: respect for difference. Difference, whether it's difference of race, religion or nationality. And the second principle is institutions. When you look at Europe, you'll find a council of ministers, all countries are there. Look at the European Commission, all countries are there. And the third principle is to work together in the common interest – social-economic development. In other words, spilling their sweat not their blood. And that breaks down the barriers of centuries. The identities of both communities are fully respected. The institutions are created in such a way that both sections of the community play a full role. (Proportional representation ensures that.) I have no doubt that in a generation or two all of that work will break down the barriers of the past and a whole new Ireland will evolve based on agreement and respect for difference.

MF: Can you speak a little about the Sunningdale Agreement 1973/74? What brought it down?

JH: The Sunningdale Agreement was brought down by opposition both from the DUP and Sinn Féin. But thirty years later when we got back to negotiate a settlement again, the problem hadn't changed, therefore neither did our approach in the SDLP to resolving it. When you look at the Good Friday agreement, it's identical. Indeed, as Seamus Mallon said on that very day that we negotiated the Good Friday Agreement, it was 'Sunningdale for slow learners'. When you look now at who is implementing the Good Friday Agreement, you'll find the parties that opposed the Sunningdale Agreement.

Seamus Heaney

Itravelled to Heaney's hometown and asked if there were any Heaney statues or memorabilia I could photograph. 'Oh you want to talk to his brother,' a woman told me. After a few attempts, I did meet Heaney's brother – but only briefly – and he referred me to another brother who he described as 'a talkin man' and, as it turned out, a true gentleman. Travelling around Heaney's townland and its hinterland, I learned that until the 1950s the Heaneys lived in a house which faced the house of 'Jim' Evans. It was just beside the crossroads where Christopher was killed on February 25th – that is why it was a 'Mid-Term Break' for the border Heaney. Then left down a bumpy road where gypsies, the Shivers, used to live. Folk neither helped nor hindered them much. Turn right at the junction and soon the pri-

mary school house, Anahorish, where Heaney went to school, is on the right. At Castledawson, a largely Protestant town nearby, there is, along a row of small houses off the centre of the town, the house of Heaney's granny. Heaney was born on Toomb Road, Mossbawn, near Castledawson. Their farm was Mossbawn. Their townland was Tampiarn. Then Heaney's father, Paddy Heaney (1910–1986), inherited sixty acres of land and they moved to Bellaghy in February, 1954. Bellaghy was more Catholic than other places in the area. I took a photo of the Protestant farm opposite Heaney's homeplace which features in a poem called 'The Other Side'.

It was in this environment that Heaney got his first schooling. Theoretically, Anahorish was a mixed school. Within its walls, however, girls and boys were taught separately. It was mixed religion-wise as well. The school's make-up is discussed in this interview. In the Bogside of Derry City, which was more harried by the security forces and naturally more politicised, the impact of the Eleven Plus was more quickly recognised. Something that should be emphasised about the Eleven Plus exam, in keeping with attitudes about education in Ireland at the time, was how arbitrarily students were chosen for the test. I spoke to one man who attended Anahorish at this time who had been in the wrong room, not in the Master's room where the boys were preparing for the Eleven Plus. 'My mother went to the teacher

and said, "put him in for the Eleven Plus, the worst he can do is fail it".' The five that the Master had earmarked to do the Eleven Plus failed. But he passed. He has often wondered since whether it was fair on him but unfair on them.

On his way to school, Heaney and his friends would chant:

'Up the long ladder and down the short rope
To hell with King Billy and God bless the Pope.'

To which the Protestant children would reply:

'Splitter splatter holy water
Scatter the Paypishes every one
If that won't do
We'll cut them in two
And give them a touch of the
Red, white and blue'. (*Preoccupations*, Faber and Faber, 1980)

Heaney's elders called him and his fellow schoolboys, aged eight and nine, 'scholars'. The old people in Heaney's area all said, 'You're going to get the learning, a pen is lighter than a spade'. It is an Irish thing to say, 'Seamus, you are an educated man ...' Most of the previous generation had left school at that age. The Eleven Plus made all the difference. It entrained a series of things: entry to grammar school, entry to university, the opening up of the professions for people who had previously been outside the loop.

On Heaney's first day at St. Columb's his mother returned home and said, 'he is sharing a cubicle with Liam Donnelly'. Liam was dapper, 'a hammered-down wee man', and came from Castledawson, though the two had never met before; the world was small before the advent of widespread car usage. Every other week Heaney's mother would send a package to Heaney in St. Columb's. Boarders shared their package of cake and other goodies with each other, so on a week that no package arrived their friends then shared with them.

The boy who sat beside Heaney on the day of the St. Columb's entrance examinations asked him where he would like to be if he was not there. Heaney replied gruffly, 'Home!' Still, boarders had to make do with being away. Boarders cultivated a parish ambiance to which day-boys were not privy. City boys regarded them as other than them, dangerous hallions. 'Their every sentence ended with a closed fist,' a city boy remembers. Boarders came from all over the province: Dungloe, Ballybuffey, Derry and Fermanagh. They had highly varied backgrounds. Heaney was occasionally *Fear an Tí don Chéilí* (the man of the house at Irish dancing sessions).

Heaney's brilliance at school often seemed in contrast to his manner – somnolent and a grin seldom far from his lips. He evinced a talent for mathematics and science. It was the focus on the humanities at St. Columb's, I believe, that helped to steer Heaney and others the literary way. Had he been born sixty years later and gone to the St. Columb's of today, he might well have become a mathematician or scientist. To some extent, St. Columb's looked down on the sciences (which would not be the case in St. Columb's today). This was a transference from British schools of the prestige in which the classics were held over science, 'the stinks'. Science facilities were very poor. Science was taught by rote: red litmus turns blue under alkaline conditions and so forth. Boys were seldom taught why such things happened.

In accordance with the emphasis in St. Columb's on the arts, S.B. O'Kelly used to bring Heaney's essays into other classes and read them aloud to students. As well as English, Heaney was always brilliant at Latin. His report cards – both at Christmas and Summer – read 80 or 90 per cent. The only subject at which he was a little weak was art.

The boys were still small children when they did the Eleven Plus and were in no way prepared for grammar school. Discipline was tight and ignorance was an offence at St. Columb's. Since boarders had four hours a night in the study hall, they wrote bags of letters home. (Heaney is still a prolific letter writer.) One boarder told me:

> 'It would be humiliating to read a letter home now. I do not want to see one. Certainly it was not six years of absolute hell. The institution reflected the way things were at home in some respects where circumstances were Spartan enough.'

When Heaney visited the Soviet Union, it reminded him of 1940s Derry: shoes were available, but black shoes only. Things were scarce. Nobody had luxuries. Many boarders speak of the first time they tasted tea in St. Columb's – it was really awful. By the end of their time there, they were used to it.

Four boys repeated senior year in a special class in 1956: Micheal Cassoni, Paddy Mullarky, Seamus Deane and Seamus Heaney. They were not, strictly speaking, too young to go to university. But their parents and teachers felt that an extra year at school would do them good. (They could use their scholarships the following year anyway.) Since there was a different syllabus in English, they attended a special class taught by Sean B. O'Kelly. They had a class of forty minutes with him three to five days a week. It had a lasting effect on Heaney.

The word 'coof', from a John Clare poem, came into usage in the class. It came to denote a fool. They read a few poems by Yeats, but Irish literature was generally regarded as lesser than English literature in the college. Jack Gallagher, another teacher of English, prided himself on teaching proper English. He would articulate, 'the lips on teeth and tip of the tongue'.

Boarders got to know each other well through living together. One boarder remembers Heaney as being very rooted:

> 'I have known nobody to change so little in the course of his life. He knows the measure of himself. He is dead sound. And he has a better memory than anyone I have ever met.'

Heaney was in fifth year when his younger brother entered St. Columb's in 1955. Heaney's presence shielded his younger brother. Heaney was then tuck shop boy and Head Prefect in his sixth year. (Deane was Head Prefect for day-boys.) Most first years had to sleep in a cubicle ('in the cubes'), as Heaney did in his first few years. Heaney's younger brother joined Heaney in a room with a boy named Brian Caffery:

> 'I had the best protection going – an older brother. In addition to Maths, I did five A levels: French, Irish, Latin, History and English. At the end of Senior/5th Year, I was sixteen years old. You had to have an average of 65 to get a scholarship to go to university. The Dean hauled me in and asked me how much I would get if I repeated. I told him I would get around 75. He told me to aim for 80. I got 74 or 75, just like I said I would. You needed 80 to get a State Exhibition.'

When his younger brother first went to unversity in 1961, aged 17, 'it was the first time I went to Belfast. Seamus drove me there.'

Intellectual prowess was prized over social ability in St. Columb's. 'Socially, I was a half-wit', remembers one former Head Prefect. (The legacy of that Head Prefect was that he abolished trashings in the library.) Senior prefects gathered in 'The Libs' (the library) on Saturday to dish out punishments on carefully selected boys. It occasionally happened that senior prefects would only punish one boy of two who had been messing, because the other was a 'friend' or a relative. Some parents never laid a glove on their children, so why would parents allow teachers to do so? The violence in St. Columb's was no secret. It was intended to give boys a notion of the order of the universe. River water flows downwards and life is tough. That had to be learned.

On going to Queen's University, Heaney paid seven and six a week at a B&B on Cable Street in Belfast which he shared with Peter Gallagher, another St. Columb's boy, for a brief period.

While at Queen's, a group including Deane and Heaney went to the Gaeltacht. In an interview later in this book, Heaney speaks of their becoming individuals through experiencing this time away. It was part of a new, self-determined education. 'I suppose I would still put trust in education. To quote Frost again: education changes the plane of regard. It helps you to get a new look at yourself' (quoted in Michael Parker's *The Making of a Poet*, Palgrave Macmillan, p. 83). The following poem highlights Heaney's 'trust in education ... to get a new look at yourself':

The Gaeltacht

'I wish, *mon vieux*, that you and Barlo and I
Were back in Rosguill, on the Atlantic Drive,
And that it was again nineteen-sixty ...
If we could see ourselves, if the people we are now
Could hear what we were saying ...'

Heaney has confirmed that '*mon vieux*' is indeed Deane. Part of the fascination for me in researching this book has been to be able to see and hear the people as they were then, in the context of the time. Notably, Heaney has written more and more about his early youth and St. Columb's as he has grown older. Yet another poem dedicated to Deane reads:

'St. Columb's College where I billeted
For six years, overlooked your Bogside.'

Another poem mentioned in the interview, 'The Border Campaign', shows an alarming shift from a portrait of the young, cocooned boarder to the violence as a result of the political border.

In addition to confidence in their intelligence, the boys needed confidence in themselves as people. Heaney had had eleven solid years at home on the farm. Irrespective of what profession he entered, he would surely have had a degree of self-respect just as he has now. 'As a member of the 11-plus generation of Catholic scholarship boys, just recently appointed to the faculty of Queen's University, [Heaney felt the] energy and confidence on the nationalist side and a developing liberalism – as well as the usual obstinacy and reaction – on the unionist side' (*Finders Keepers*, Faber and Faber).

In one of the poems Heaney reads, 'The Canton of Expectation', he includes the mummified phrase, 'not in our lifetime', that Northern Catholics used to describe their political heritage. It was an end of the rainbow aspiration to a re-unified Ireland. The phrase is still being used. Just as 'our people in the North' is now much less used in the south, so the phrase 'not in our lifetime' seems to become more an aspiration than a realistic goal with every generation. 'The Canton of Expectation' traces the growth away from abstention from the Stormont Parliament and the use of empty phrases into 'the new age of demands'. It is unsurprising that Heaney's poetry was commended for its ethical depth by the Nobel Prize Committee. Coulter is right when he says that the history of this era was made by the Austin Curries and the John Humes who represented their people when they made those demands.

On the morning after Heaney won the Nobel Prize in 1995, a *Guardian* journalist arrived at Heaney's brother's back door to ask what he thought of the fact that his brother had won the Nobel Prize. The brother replied, 'it is the best thing since Derry won the All-Ireland'. (Derry won the All-Ireland in 1993.)

Despite all his achievements, Heaney remains very rooted. Late one night in a pub in Derry City, I met a man who was caretaker at St. Columb's. He told me that when a book about the college was produced no mention was made of the caretaker who had served the college for decades, and during the period in question. His successor was disappointed at the omission. The caretaker during the 1950s in St. Columb's had woken up at five in the morning to light fires to heat the college. He worked tirelessly to keep St. Columb's in good shape. So the new caretaker pointed out the omission to the writers of the book, 'just to get it off my chest'. That former caretaker's name was Jim Logue. He was not forgotten by Heaney who wrote a poem in his memory.

MF: What sort of primary school education did you get?

SH: My first schooling occurred forty miles from St. Columb's College in Anahorish School: four teachers in four classrooms. It was a four teacher school. The teachers arrived on bicycles. It was basically a kind of nineteenth century school still operating in the mid-twentieth century. It was under Catholic management, but was actually a mixed school. The enrolment had a lot of the local Protestant families involved: the Dixons, the Smiths, the Ewarts, the Ellises, the Clarks, the Boals. There wasn't any poisonous sense of sectarianism. This was the countryside, it wasn't the ghettoised city. Of course, those families left at the Catechism time. My best friend who lived across the road was Tommy Evans, also a Protestant. It was a country of community as well as a country of divisions. I was supposed to be smart, so the master put me in for the Eleven Plus exam. I got the Eleven Plus.

MF: What was the reaction when you passed the Eleven Plus?

SH: I do remember Master Murphy calling the class round the desk and taking a half crown out of his pocket and saying, 'Now this is for this man here, he has got the scholarship and he's going away to Derry, so

this is for him getting the exam'. That was a kind of a memory-marking moment. And St. Columb's College was forty miles away. First time I'd crossed the mountain. It was soul-marking, the day I came to Derry with my father and mother.

MF: What do you remember of your first day?

SH: We went in and met the president and signed in. That was in the afternoon at about three or four o'clock. You didn't officially have to be in until seven o'clock, so we drove to Buncrana and they bought me a Conway Stuart pen. I always remember that twelve and sixpence fountain pen. That was a kind of initiation into the higher condition. You had a fountain pen now. But of course what I remember most about that day was the moment when they had to leave. They walked down the path towards the gates, and that really was a very homesick, sad moment of loss. I'll never forget that. What I also remember is the first weekend, the first Halloween break. It would also be 1951. At the end of the weekend at home, I went out to the bus stop at the end of our lane. I think I was crying my eyes out and my mother was with me. There was a neighbour of ours, Mrs McNicholl. She spoke very frankly, and she said to my mother, 'You're an old bitch,' she said, 'sending that child away like that, crying'. One of my happiest memories is being on the riverbank the summer before St. Columb's. It was only recently that I realised my father was probably thinking: he's going away. Just being together on the riverbank and not saying much is a form of communion that is very special. So father and son like that, it allowed something to happen and flow quietly. Happiness.

MF: You wrote once of returning home on your first holiday and said that it was your 'first meeting with your mother as other'.

SH: We came back from Derry City as far as Magherafelt in a special private college bus, then I went on what they called the service bus: the UTA, Ulster Transport Authority bus. So I would be waiting, usually, in the waiting room. The first time I came home, my mother walked in. Years later I thought to myself, well obviously she knew I was coming home for that while and just wanted to see me first, because it was a small house and there was a big crowd of us at the time. I guess she wanted that little while on her own with me. Sons and lovers ...

MF: What are your first memories of St. Columb's?

SH: Just the sense of regimentation, and the first day in the big study (I've written about it), the terror of the strap. Everybody was lined up. I'd never seen such execution, such executive strapping as happened that day. That first day there was a definite sense of scare, really. You had come from a home and suddenly you were in an institution. I was homesick for weeks, and very vulnerable and didn't know the ropes. Weeping, internally weeping, but holding the line.

MF: You were always conscious of St. Columb's being religious?

SH: If you took Greek it meant that you felt you had a vocation for the priesthood. If you took French it meant you were opting for what they then called 'the world'. I chose French. Still, the fact of the matter is that we were in a religious institution. We began the morning with Mass, we ended the day with night prayers – the whole ethos of the place was religious.

MF: Did being away at school make you feel separate from your family?

SH: My brother Pat came to St. Columb's after me, and my brother Dan also. But I was the first to go away. There was no alienation, but there was a sense that I was headed for a different destination from the ones at home.

MF: You wrote movingly of the 'border campaign', the 1956-62 IRA campaign. What do you remember about that time?

SH: There was an IRA campaign in the 1950s. Newspapers weren't available to us

in St. Columb's. Crystal radios were also forbidden, even though you might be able to construct one and listen to it under the sheets. Basically, you were in quarantine. But you did hear of this: there was a bomb or something in Magherafelt. I do remember arriving on that south Derry bus, seeing Magherafelt Courthouse as we came in, with scorch marks and a hole in the roof. This sense that it had been, as I say, attacked. And the word 'attack', which was so abstract until that moment, gained a new reality – suddenly you realised this was dangerous. This was the first time outside of newsreels or books or photographs that evidence of destructive intent was present.

MF: You have very fond memories of your English teacher, S.B. O'Kelly.

SH: I remember well the books I read with Sean B. O'Kelly, the authors I read in sixth form, especially. We had a very special class, four of us – Seamus Deane, Paddy Mullarkey, Michael Cassoni and myself, four people. It was almost like a first year university seminar for us. The authors I read with him I got to know by heart: Wordsworth, Chaucer, Shakespeare, Thomas Hardy and so on were important ever after. But

O'Kelly had an inwardness with his subject. He could have been a university teacher. He had a sensibility as well as a scholarly sense of the material. And he was an educationalist, a natural communicator. He was eccentric also, of course, that was important. One of his nicknames was Honk. Naturally all the teachers were mythologised by us, but O'Kelly especially. He had a long, loping stride that we used to imitate.

MF: Is it fair to say that there was a focus on the humanities over the sciences at St. Columb's?

SH: These colleges were diocesan seminaries, so Greek and Latin had to be taught. There was a kind of humanist emphasis on languages, definitely. One of my big regrets is that I didn't proceed with history. I could have read history afterwards, but I think if you do a subject at school it aims you and gives you an entrée in a special way.

MF: What effect did boarding have on you? How well or badly did it prepare you for university?

SH: People used to say that being a boarder made a man of you. You were able to stand up for yourself and so on, which is true enough actually. I was cauterised over that five or six years. You didn't allow yourself to trust emotionally. The world had changed radically, leaving home, going there. But when we went to Queen's, we were a kind of gang. St. Columb's boys sat together. And then there was the ever entrancing and fascinating new development of being close to girls: very demure it was in those days. There was a kind of giggly convent girl/college boy tryout. There was the Irish Society, the Gaelic Football Society. Those things broke down on – sectarian is too strong a word – religious division lines or social lines. The following will tell you something about the Eleven Plus Catholic Generation. There was a Catholic chaplain, a man called Michael Kelly, and there used to be sodality meetings every week with a homily and a reading and benediction. But the little homily on one occasion consisted of advice to us not to be sticking to the Gaelic Football Club and the Irish Society; to join the Rowing Club and to move out, in order to become middle class Catholics, not to be scooting back into the ghetto and into the south Derry bus. That was indicative of what was on the cards at that time for that generation. Move out and join up. Don't skulk in the corner. Show your mettle.

MF: You once meditated on American TV that your childhood would have been much different had you grown up on the Falls Road, pitted against the (Protestant) Shankill. Could you speak a little about that?

SH: Well, my own house was mercifully free of sectarian attitude. I've often connected it with my father being out on the road in the cattle trade. A lot of the people who came to the house, friends of his, were, well, Orangemen. But the Catholic/Protestant thing was handled cheerfully and capably, and mockingly. That didn't mean it wasn't for real, but you were being given a lesson in good conduct. To be truthful, that's what's called for. You're not going to eliminate deep-seated loyalty and sectarian attitude if it's there. But if good conduct prevails, we'll have come a great distance. It was learnt in the conditions that we lived in.

MF: Did you find the Derry City boys whom you encountered in St. Columb's to be much more politically astute?

SH: The St. Columb's Derry City people were much more alert to the politicised sectarian, Loyalist/Republican dimension of things, much more vigilant and active, activist even, yeah. Much more sardonic.

MF: How was it to be a Catholic teaching at Queen's?

SH: In the mid to late sixties the faculty, the teaching staff of Queen's, was mostly (certainly much more than they are now) British academics, usually on their way somewhere else. They were not clued in to the under-life of the society. There was a kind of liberal, cheerful, slightly antiseptic atmosphere, which is as good a way as any I suppose of handling a septic condition.

Still, I remember feeling that I had done something unusual in my first year teaching, teaching James Joyce. We were very bird-mouthed about all of those religious and political matters in the sixties, and I remember feeling I had shocked the class a wee bit by saying, 'Do you think it matters if you're a Catholic or a Protestant when you read James Joyce?' Those realities were very tenderly present and uneasy. I think that my generation in the academy broke some silences. Nothing drastic, but we broke that little bit of silence and made that little bit of space. We let people talk a bit about what was there, albeit through literature. I believe teaching can effect small changes.

You could perceive yourself as a generation about ten years afterwards, when you looked around at the people who had been in your class at school. Some of them were lawyers, some of them were politicians. Austin Currie I knew at Queen's and Seamus Deane and Patrick Mullarkey. John Hume I had also known at St. Columb's. He was a day-boy. He used to come into the big study in the evenings. He was marked for distinction, you felt always, because he was the first day-boy who was given the privilege to come into the boarders' study. That was a distinction indeed. Later on, there was a sense of all those people on the move, voices being heard and positions being taken. Entering the professions and being part of the swim. It was good.

MF: This was the moment that the first generation was coming through. How was that manifest?

SH: In those days, the unionist community were in possession of the ball. They had a sense of ownership of the ground, not only the ground but the professions. The nationalists thought, well, we don't accept what's here. They tended to stand apart, have an abstentionist attitude. I think that the Eleven Plus brought people into acceptance because they began to say, okay, we're now part of it. I was part of Queen's. I was part of official Northern Ireland culture. I was in the university. Aware of some kind of representative status. My experience was different from, I think, Seamus Deane's, who went back to Derry, taught in Derry, did an MA, then went to Cambridge, and after Cambridge went to America. But I had re-entered the establishment in Belfast. I knew the BBC producers. I knew Sam Hanna Bell, John Boyd. I was in and out of the BBC. I was in and out of the Arts Council, in and out of the art galleries, in and out of Queen's. When I stopped, it was only because the writing carried me towards a sense that it was time for me to break out and be a writer myself.

MF: So what impact did 1947 have?

SH: The scholarship became available on merit after the 1947 Education Act. The difference that the Education Act and the Eleven Plus made was that people with merit, with intelligence, were given the scholarship, so that talent brought forward a whole new set of people. That arrival into the adult population, eventually, of educated people from the working class, from farming backgrounds, brought a new kind of critical intelligence, a new kind of appetite for excellence into play. They had a sense of adventure, a sense of themselves as a generation with some sense of possibility and advantage and renewal. They were aware of the people who hadn't got the advantages in their family and among their neighbours. They were political in that they had a strong sense of being responsible. You can see that certainly in Hume and Austin Currie.

MF: Did you succeed because of or in spite of St. Columb's?

SH: I'm not sure. A lot of the formation I had there was just reformation of what was in me from home. The movement was from sorrow to certitude, to some kind of independence or individuation. I think that's true.

MF: You were sent to sit in the college sick-bay on the morning your brother died. St. Columb's must have seemed a particularly antiseptic place at that time?

SH: The morning that I heard about Christopher's accident I was serving Mass. It used to be a kind of privilege to go across to serve Mass in the Nazareth House: you got a warm breakfast. I was coming up the walks towards the front of the college. I was brought up to the president's room, and told about Christopher having been knocked down and killed. After that I was brought over to the sick bay. I just waited there, and I was of course sad and stricken, a lost child really, and eventually I was driven home. We passed a little field that day in the car. For years and years afterwards when I passed that field I noticed it and it always brought back that moment.

Mid-Term Break

I sat all morning in the college sick bay
Counting bells knelling classes to a close.
At two o'clock our neighbors drove me home.

In the porch I met my father crying –
He had always taken funerals in his stride –
And Big Jim Evans saying it was a hard blow.

The baby cooed and laughed and rocked the pram
When I came in, and I was embarrassed
By old men standing up to shake my hand

And tell me they were 'sorry for my trouble,'
Whispers informed strangers I was the eldest,
Away at school, as my mother held my hand

In hers and coughed out angry tearless sighs.
At ten o'clock the ambulance arrived
With the corpse, stanched and bandaged by the nurses.

Next morning I went up into the room. Snowdrops
And candles soothed the bedside; I saw him
For the first time in six weeks. Paler now,

Wearing a poppy bruise on his left temple,
He lay in the four foot box as in his cot.
No gaudy scars, the bumper knocked him clear.

A four foot box, a foot for every year.

MF: You feel that St. Columb's gave you access to a long monastic tradition that helped to give a mythic dimension to your own personal experience. Could you elaborate a little on that?

SH: The St. Columb's College experience for boarders was basically the experience of European Christian civilisation from AD 400 to AD 1940 or 50. Those institutions where life was regulated by the bell. There was basically a religious pattern to the life. The canonical shape of the day was preserved in study and the chapel and in the refectory. To have known that is to have partaken in a deep sense in historical European civilisation. That's a rather grand way of putting it, but it's true.

MF: How was it, returning to the college today?

SH: I wrote a poem a while back called 'In the Afterlife', and imagined that instead of being in the Elysian fields, I'd be walking behind Jim Logue, who was the caretaker when he was brushing the corridors and going into the haunted absent places like the old refectory and the old corridors. This would be a posthumous, ghostly life, totally familiar and at the same time totally strange. That was my experience coming in here today, walking down that corridor. [He reads]:

Bodies and Souls

1 In the Afterlife

It will be like following Jim Logue, the caretaker,
As he goes to sweep our hair off that classroom floor
Where the school barber set up once a fortnight,
Falling into step as he does his rounds,
Glimmerman of dorms and silent landings,
Of the refectory with its solid, crest-marked delph,
The ground-floor corridor, the laundry pile
And boots tagged for the cobbler. Was that your name
On a label? Were you a body or a soul?

MF: Would you mind reading 'The Canton of Expectation' as well?

SH: [He reads]: From 'The Canton of Expectation'

1

We lived deep in a land of optative moods,
under high, banked clouds of resignation.
A rustle of loss in the phrase Not in our lifetime,
the broken nerve when we prayed Vouchsafe or Deign,
were creditable, sufficient to the day.

Once a year we gathered in a field
of dance platforms and tents where children sang
songs they had learned by rote in the old language.
An auctioneer who had fought in the brotherhood
enumerated the humiliations
we always took for granted, but not even he
considered this, I think, a call to action.
Iron-mouthed loudspeakers shook the air
yet nobody felt blamed. He had confirmed us.
When our rebel anthem played the meeting shut
we turned for home and the usual harassment
by militiamen on overtime at roadblocks.

2

And the next thing, suddenly, this change of mood.
Books open in the newly wired kitchens.
Young heads that might have dozed a life away
against the flanks of milking cows were busy
paving and pencilling their first causeways
across the prescribed texts. The paving stones
of quadrangles came next and a grammar
of imperatives, the new age of demands.
They would banish the conditional for ever,
this generation born impervious to
the triumph in our cries of de profundis.
Our faith in winning by enduring most
they made anathema, intelligences
brightened and unmannerly as crowbars.

3

What looks the strongest has outlived its term.
The future lies with what's affirmed from under.
These things that corroborated us when we dwelt
under the aegis of our stealthy patron,
the guardian angel of passivity,
now sink a fang of menace in my shoulder.
I repeat the word 'stricken' to myself
and stand bareheaded under the banked clouds
edged more and more with brassy thunderlight.
I yearn for hammerblows on clinkered planks,
the uncompromised report of driven thole-pins,
to know there is one among us who never swerved
from all his instincts told him was right action,
who stood his ground in the indicative,
whose boat will lift when the cloudburst happens.

[Optative, according to the OED, means 'of a mood of verbs, especially in Greek, expressing a wish, equivalent in meaning to English let's or if only'].

MF: You see that as the development of Northern Ireland?

SH: Yes. Three stages of development of the political scene.

MF: An allegory?

SH: Very much an allegory. First, of the anti-partition attitude, you know, the stand-off: don't go to Stormont, go to the Fheis attitude. And then, the next phase: civil rights, the age of demands, no more concessions, no more, 'sorry now'. And then, phase three, the aftermath of that: the age of violence and danger, the word 'stricken', the thunder light. Then a yearning for escape into integrity for the indicative rather than conditional, straightforward dealing. The boat will lift when the cloudburst happens. The poem says, you'll have crisis and some kind of – not Armageddon – but awful outbreak. At the same time you'll maybe come through to something better. It's Noah escaping the flood.

MF: Do you think it was your generation who accomplished that?

SH: No, no, I don't think it was our generation that accomplished it. Our generation was swamped in the nineteen-seventies, eighties and nineties. I think of myself as the sixties generation, fifties maybe, more fifties than sixties, I suppose. My sense in the sixties was that things were changing in Northern Ireland. We were part of the change which was political; we were giving articulation; things were on the move. Well, then things hotted up and changed drastically. And that amelioration notion changed into something much more revolutionary. Gradual amelioration was out; melodrama and danger were in.

Seamus Deane

An essay entitled 'Why Bogside?' (1971) embodies much of Deane's thinking on the subject of the foundation of Ulster as a political entity, and how that history impinged on the Derry of his youth. He traces the apparatus of domination of the unionist state from the lives of Catholic servants hired out to big Protestant estates in the early days of the Northern Irish State, through to the baton-charge of the St. Patrick's Day Parade in 1951 (Protestant pageantry, on the other hand, was allowed to flourish) and finally through to 5 October 1968, the first civil rights march. Deane manages, remarkably well, to show his part of Derry as a microcosm of the North.

The most important aspect of the essay is its attempt to unmask the idealism that veiled the cynical politics which Bogsiders encountered for so long. 'As soon as sectarianism is *seen* [italics mine] to be the basis upon which many Protestants accept unnecessary poverty (and thereby also uphold the grotesquely large property holdings of this small group of families), then the feudal basis of Unionism will have vanished.'

Deane's interview advocates the view that the groundbreaking education available enabled some of the brutality and cruelty that took place. According to school lore, a boy in Senior A Level Class in St. Columb's during the 1950s, McCabe, turned the tables, if only for a moment. A notoriously violent teacher is supposed to have met his nemesis in McCabe. The teacher sneered at McCabe for getting an answer wrong, saying, 'what would you know – your mother is a factory girl'. McCabe rose from his seat and sent the priest flying to the ground with a punch. The priest shouted for the President, but the boy was already on his way out the door, saying 'never mind the President, I'll never set foot in this place again'. Education was their only opportunity in life and it cost McCabe dear to make that stand. If the education of Northern Catholics constituted a sort of prison-break, the alternative was also wrenching.

With the entry to St. Columb's of the 'Eleven Plus Generation', teachers and priests were losing their authority even as they sought to exert it. One priest used to give boys 39.5 per cent in exams. The ritual was that boys then had to supplicate to the teacher for a pass grade. If the teacher thought the boy sufficiently humble, he would award a pass.

In this interview, Deane's melancholy reflection – that his childhood was happy until he came to St. Columb's – is indeed an indictment of the effect of the violent practice within its walls. Although violence permeated this society, it may come as a surprise to some that Derry City in the 1950s was a reasonably placid place, relative to what came later. The violence latent in the society had yet to come to the fore.

The class snobbery, which was so much a part of St. Columb's after 1947, had at its root a fear that the school could not absorb the change brought by the 'Eleven Plus Generation'. One priest, for example, had a row in his classroom which he called 'Nailor's Row'. It denoted the lowest of the low: a row of gurriers whom he held in the lowest esteem.

(Nailor's Row in Derry was a row of poor housing, tenements that actually faced into the wall of Derry – a murky area to live at the best of times.) Some boys saw others suffer and, because of their sensitivity, absorbed the hurt themselves. And the hurt was often publicised. Another priest provided baby teeth (soother-type sweets) to any boy who would cry when he dished out his punishments.

A teacher once gratuitously beat a boy named Gerard. Gerard had been sent into another teacher's class to borrow chalk. John spotted his older brother enter. Someone in the class roared something. The teacher turned and assumed that Gerard had said it. He gave him three on each hand. The roar went up again. The teacher assumed the same and gave him more on each palm. The boy named John was caught in a very difficult situation: to rat on the boy in class who was framing his brother or to let his brother take raps. It was excruciating. Two unwritten codes of conduct cancelled each other out. Two codes dialectically in tension, one with the other, seemed to forever occupy the boys' minds in St. Columb's. For example, it was punishable for day-boys to smuggle food in for boarders. On the other hand, the half-starved older boarders meted out their own brand of rough justice to day-boys who failed to deliver the same. (Boarders, often coming of farming stock and used to hard knocks on the GAA pitch, were by and large more robust than their day-boy counterparts.) Naturally, not all boarders were large in stature. One small boy in John's class used to wet the bed and cried himself to sleep. He was tortured for it by the other boys every night.

That said, day-boys did sometimes give food out of genuine sympathy. However poor areas like the Bogside were, there would be warm food on the table – maybe even an Ulster Fry – for dinner. Day-boys worked to a three-thirty daily afternoon release from St. Columb's. Boarders, who might not have been home for an eight week stretch, were undernourished and were often intensely miserable.

At one point, Deane's mother had four boys at St. Columb's simultaneously. She saw in her boys' faces a sign of the change to come. She belonged to a generation that felt betrayed by the drawing of the border outside Derry City, a city with a strong Donegal heritage. (The inclusion of Derry in Northern Ireland is attributable, in the main, to the fact that the Siege of Derry is iconic in the Protestant calendar.) They were disappointed by middle class Catholics on both sides of the bor-

der: the middle class in the
Republic seemed to regard the
Northern Catholic working
class as one of the lost tribes
of Israel; as might be inferred
from the attitudinising of St.
Columbs, the middle class
in the North were content to
distance themselves from areas
like the Bogside. So working
class Catholics were damned
on both sides of the border
in a sort of pincer movement.
This was also part of the reason

why the youth looked abroad for their exemplars (Deane has published a
book entitled *Foreign Affections*). It was out of this ambiance that a comment like Eamonn McCann's about the SDLP – 'middle-aged, middle-
class and middle-of-the-road' – came. It was also out of this milieu that
two of Ireland's most important socialist thinkers emerged.

The majority in the Bogside had neither a vote nor formal education. But they sensed that unionist domination in the North would
hit a wall when solicitors, journalists and politicians started to emerge
from the Catholic working class. This meant that entire systems like
the Credit Union could be formulated and run solely by Catholics. The
monolith of unionism had entered its twilight. While Deane's mother's
sons were at school, not a day passed without her saying out loud or
under her breath, 'this will break them'. How right she was. The confluence of economic stagnation and educational reform paved the way for
the next generation of Catholics to take the lead in the province. Hopes,
dreams and prayers of generations were concentrated by the 1947 Education Act; finally, the cycle of Northern Ireland could be broken. The
people who had kept previous generations down would not keep their
children down.

This generation of Northern Irish Catholics speak of where they
come from in terms of both geography and conditioning. When Heaney
writes that they 'lived in a land of optative moods', he refers primarily to

conditioning. Likewise, Deane wrote of the position of the Bogside as being 'below and between' – they were below the middle-class housing of Marlborough; between the Creggan and the Protestant town. That external conditioning was as much a part of what was home as what happened in the Bogside itself.

The modernity of Derry in the 1950s resulted from a series of foiled continuities: the cult of a dominant masculinity had been expected to continue, but it was undercut by massive unemployment and the in-dignity that went with it; the authority of the church was beginning to crumble; unionist domination was also beginning to be undermined. In the absence of these continuities or traditions, Derry people, par-ticularly students at St. Columb's, took their standards from abroad. As a young man, Deane was part of the Wolfe Tone Club. Its focus on international movements and events informed upon Deane's socialism.

During Deane's first week in school Tom Mullarky and McLivery got into a fight at St. Columb's. Jack 'Rusty' Gallagher, the English teacher, made every boy in the class write a poem about it. Deane's intellect was focused on English. He was intense and very well-read. A talented right-footer, he was the best footballer in the school with a ten-nis ball. Deane's brother Liam was less skillful but 'he was tough – after playing football with Liam, you'd be counting your ankles', as a class-mate remembers. Deane and his brothers were all good soccer players. Younger brother Gerard was also a tough player. (Gerard, as they say in Derry, would have kicked his granny.)

Some teachers like Jack 'Rusty' Gallagher and Sean B. O'Kelly were civilised and civilising forces in the school – they sought out the opin-ion of the boys, and that was revolutionary. Other exceptional teachers included Father Kelly (Spiritual Director), Father Hanny (Geography) and Father McGlinchey (Classics). The younger teachers tended to be nice. Corkery Dunbar never laid a glove on anybody. Teachers of a gen-tler persuasion encountered heavy opposition over their passive ways. John Hume and James Sharkey were of a similar stamp when they be-came teachers at St. Columb's. Students were so used to being petrified that they tended to take advantage if a teacher respected them. But Gallagher and O'Kelly were strong enough in and of themselves to keep control of students. A young teacher, employing this tactic, fared less well.

That said, the civility of such teachers could hardly eclipse the misdeeds of the martinets. The tortures of one priest at St. Columb's are too many to enumerate: one snowy morning he decided that he wanted a snowman and promptly sent a boy out to stand in the snow; on discovering that a boy in his class thought he had discovered a mathematical short-cut on a sum, he told him to leave the class by jumping out the window – the quickest way. The teacher is sent up in Deane's *Reading in the Dark*. As comes through in this interview, the tiny perversions and miseries that existed in St. Columb's can scarcely be revealed through anecdote alone, much as the anecdote may be amusing in retrospect. What distinguishes Deane's testimony is his willingness to engage with other colonial narratives such as the writings of Frantz Fanon – histories that show where a society has unsound grounding its institutions will also be unstable.

Father McGlinchey was a superb classics teacher and he gave extra time to students. He instilled Deane with enthusiasm for the subject and ambition. A schoolmate once asked the young Deane what he would like to be when he grew up. He replied that he wanted to be a Professor of English Literature. Reminiscing on the eccentricity of this teacher, Deane said he

> 'actually wept – if you didn't understand a line of Virgil. "Cannot you see this ... oh" and then he would go to the window and take in big breaths to control his emotion or he'd go into fits of laughter and puns. We would be looking at each other, sort of saying: "this nutter". But, at the same time, we were glad to be in his class rather than with the Irish teacher, having your fingers chopped off' (*Journal of Irish Studies*, Japan, Vol. 21).

Later in life, having become a scholar in his own right, Deane comes to see that the teaching of classics at St. Columb's lacked an important political dimension because of the colonial condition of the North.

Priests had by no means a monopoly on violence. Lay teachers from the Republic were often just as brutal and their tactics did not endear students to the Free State. Only the old or small teachers did not mete out beatings. There was no accountability, no regulation, no justification – just constant violence. (Deane once witnessed a boy have his eardrum burst by a teacher.) There was an assumption that teachers were entitled to this power. Many did not really apply themselves to teaching or encourage those with ability. One teacher, for example, declared at the beginning of the year that 'I do not move from here'. He would remain, for the most part, at the front of the class. If any boy in the back row acted up, he would lash the boy nearest to him. Then he would say, 'you see x for that after class'. Thus he cultivated violence between boys and took enjoyment in delegating it.

That violence was an integral part of the system of Northern Irish society is doubtless. As described in his interview later in the book, Paul Brady's violent relationship with the bully who never laid a hand on him somehow symbolises the violence smouldering in Northern Ireland in the 1950s before it exploded. In such a violent society, revolutionary change rather than therapy is required, as Deane argues. Education was a crucible of self-development. Education, the transcendental weapon, was favoured over real weapons. 'To break the unionist state there were two weapons available: guns or education ...' (Interview with Seamus Deane by John Brown, *In the Chair*, Salmon Poetry). Heaney also wrote a poem, using these two alternatives in a simile: 'The squat pen rests/ snug as a gun' ('Digging', in *Death of a Naturalist*, Faber and Faber). They had the government's milk but the policeman's baton.

While this education was violent, violence depended on the personality of the teacher. When teachers arrived in the college, they felt that they had to establish a reputation. In those days, it showed considerable humanity to refrain from corporal punishment. There were interplays between Derry City boys and Derry teachers, petty resentments that were not always open. Bitterness built, but the teachers represented an institution. Deane's commentary on institutional violence is an important contribution to this history. The word violence, or one of its derivatives, appears numerous times in Deane's interview. As one past pupil quipped, 'they have dissolved Guantanomo Bay, but St. Columb's remains intact'.

On leaving St. Columb's, a group including Heaney and Deane 'went up' to Belfast. Laurence Lerner taught as a tutor in the history department and he encouraged Deane to write essays on the Balkans. Deane and Heaney had the same digs for a year, beside Ravenhill Road. After Queen's, Deane became a teacher for a period in Derry. Like many small cities, it is easy to stay in Derry and become complacent. Instead, he left his teaching job and went to Cambridge to do a PhD. Deane otherwise could have 'caught the Derry disease' and stayed at home. 'Com'st thou smiling from the world's snare uncaught?' (*Anthony and Cleopatra* 4.8.17-18).

On Limewood Street, where Seamus Deane grew up, the houses are very small, built on a precarious slant. But today they are prosperous looking. The street is just a drop-kick to the Celtic Bar on the corner which overlooks the Brandywell Stadium. Graffitti on the nearby walls tell Shinners to go away (the Protestant Fountainside still clings to its own Pied Pipers). Hamas and the Palestinian flag seem to have supplanted Sinn Féin and the Tricolour in the Bogside.

MF: Where were you born?

SD: I was born in Derry here in what is now called (since the Troubles) the Bogside, in an area which was very severely deprived in all sorts of ways, but in which I was perfectly happy. I was forever finding a way to try and scrape a few pennies together through selling jam jars: a large jam jar was worth 3p, a small jam jar was worth 1p. With 3p you could go to the cinema. The City Cinema in William Street was quite risky. A standard trick was to have somebody from behind you suddenly clamp your shoulders – while your shoulders and arms were being held, another guy would rub chewing gum into your hair.

In some ways it was a grinding existence, but in other ways I enjoyed it until one became aware – and very, very quickly – of the police. There was a police station in the middle of the Bogside then, and the police were always a menace. As they continued to be and continue to be.

MF: What are your earliest memories of that?

SD: I suppose one of my first memories was a vivid memory involving the policing [in 1951] of a St Patrick's Day march down Shipquay Street, a rather straggly affair. Eddie McAteer was holding the banner or flag at the front. The police lined up at the bottom of Shipquay Street and baton-charged. I ran into the Palace cinema, hid behind the kiosk. That was the occasion on which (up on The Wall) a photograph was taken by a *Derry Journal* photographer of a policeman batoning or arching over a tiny little girl who could have been no more than five or six. That photograph I remember was sent to all the Dublin newspapers and the London newspapers. But the only newspaper that published it, other than the *Derry Journal*, was the *Manchester Guardian*. That was the first time I felt just how closed off we were; that there was no chance of having the injustice of the Protestant sectarian state or its militant and paramilitary apparatus exposed. Most especially disappointing was that no one in Dublin was interested in revealing anything about this. Incidents like that emphasised a degree of isolation. We, as a community, felt isolated within, if you like, a ring of Catholic middle class houses, which were higher up the hill – we were at the base of the valley. And we felt isolated within Derry as a majority which was politically lamed by gerrymander and housing discrimination. In a series of concentric circles, the wider you went, the more remote your community was from any contact with power or justice.

That sense of isolation tightened the community's sense of inner bonding, tightened it to a point that was always bordering on the unhealthy. Yet it was happy. Until I came to school, it was a happy childhood.

MF: Things changed dramatically when you arrived in St. Columb's?

SD: I came here in '51. I came to secondary school at the age of ten, after the '47 Act was passed. The college didn't exactly open sunlit fields for you. It meant possibly you would get some kind of education. Many priests obviously realised too late that they really shouldn't have been priests. They realised also they shouldn't have been teachers. But there they were, priest-teachers. They were trapped in a situation which here was made all the worse by the fact that there was this sudden influx of scholarship boys who not only brought a numbers problem. Discipline was more of an issue than it might have been.

MF: How did that become known to you?

SD: It was made obvious to some of us by some of the teachers that to be from the Bogside, to be from the working class, was a distinct disadvantage; that we shouldn't be here. I remember being shocked a priest could be capable of such cheap injustice. There were more serious forms of injustice that they were capable of (as we learned as the years went by). Part of the problem for me at St. Columb's was to wonder, is this place like others? Or is this extraordinarily pressured? You could find in schoolboys' literature where physical beatings and various forms of snobbery and various forms of official misery were the rule. You had the usual ideology there about being hardened by school for the world beyond, the way our hands were hardened by being slapped. If we soaked them in vinegar it made them harder, so that the skin was shiny and tough. Leather straps would bounce off them. Unless the teacher took the trouble, as he often did, to make sure that the leather strap licked up on to the more delicate skin on the wrist, which vinegar didn't harden.

The trouble they went to exert their authority through all sorts of conceivable mini-tortures such as using a sliding blackboard as a guillotine; making boys hold their fingers in a pyramid and then beating the pyramid of fingers with the wooden side of a duster; trying to make the so-called tough boys cry and then regarding it as a triumph if the boy broke down.

It was not just the priests. When it came to the psychotics, the priests and the lay people were almost evenly divided. Everybody thought it was worse that a priest should be like this. I used to gaze at these guys and wondered, what is going on? These people are not interested in teaching. I got a good Latin education here, but I remember one priest, who was the Dean of the college, Father McCauley, who taught Latin. He was incompetent. I thought, what is this man doing here? Why is he teaching Latin? Couldn't they have him washing the chasubles or something useful? This is a strange structure in which there are some brilliant teachers and civilised men. And there are others who are on sort of a crime rampage called a teaching career.

But this injustice is not revealed simply through this anecdote or that. All in this city were political amputees. Everybody was powerless in some sense, and the powerless who looked at those who had power – they looked at the unionist government, the police force and the Special Powers Act and the discrimination and the whole repertoire of oppression – and assumed that power and authority were the same thing. The policeman with his belt and baton and revolver, and the priest with his Roman collar. These were two uniforms that bestowed power. The priest should have known that he had a power in the Roman collar which should not have been the power of coercion (which the other one was). His should have been that of persuasion. They ruined their real authority by relying on the strap, which was their baton. I think the more powerless people are, and the more they imitate unjust power, then the more inclined they become to those little perversions of power which actually undermine any notion of what authority could truly be. The person who had authority over you was the person who could hit you. There would be no redress, no way of coming back at it. If you struck a teacher, you were expelled forthwith. And there was nowhere for you to go, and of course we were in Derry, we were in the western part of Northern Ireland, where the unemployment rates were terrifying. I think the official rate in Derry was over 20 per cent. But in fact there were areas like the Bogside, the lower Creggan, where the male unemployment rate was well over 50, 60 per cent. Unemployment was the condition to which most people before our generation had been doomed. So if your education was aborted by doing something like hitting a teacher, you were out.

MF: Can you say a little more about the source of the violence?

SD: The source of the kind of violence that we became acclimatised to – you did become acclimatised to it and one part of you always had a sense of outrage, but the rest of you felt this is normal – was the structure of dominance then in place. You knew that the whole point of the structure was to produce a form of domination that made you perfectly obedient. That's why I understood some of the beatings in class. It wasn't to teach somebody some element of a subject. It was to teach you that you were a subject, and that you were subject to a system of domination which wanted actually to claim that it was a system of authority that should be respected. Nobody ever accused the authorities or the communities in Northern Ireland of being charming or endearing, appealing to people so that they would behave spontaneously in accord with rules.

The whole point of obedience was to make people recognise that they were subjects; there was no attempt to disguise this; obedience was demanded, subjugation was the naked condition; late capitalism still had to arrive with its preferred narcotic form of subjugation, which many people feel to be, in contrast, almost like freedom. The only institutional form of authority that we were supposed to give allegiance to was not the state but the church, even though the church could be said to have been hand in glove with the state. Nevertheless, there was an important distinction. The belief in the church became a form of resentment at yet another tough form of authority, and that intensified as people came to the school. The church unwittingly committed a form of political suicide because it brutally revealed its alliance with all sorts of other things, which were officially not Christian, not as such – like the class prejudices of the teachers. One teacher whose father was a Papal Knight, Father Coulter was his name, several times waved the *Times Literary Supplement* in front of us, saying, 'this is a paper you boys will never read'.

There were a lot of eccentrics, and there were a lot of drunks, quiet drunks. This was a system of authority that was changing itself into a system of power, and doing that mistakenly under the aegis of the Socialist Government's Education Act. They couldn't handle the effect of that legislation. The Roman Catholic Church couldn't remain what it had been; once they had to teach the working classes, their class prejudice revealed itself. Every one of them was anxious nevertheless to exert authority, reproducing the structures of domination that the state had used; mass education exposed a church that had won respect from being oppressed. The myth of the priest could not survive his becoming a teacher in a strenuous situation. So it was sort of a melancholy place in that respect, made the more so by the excellence of some of the very good teachers.

MF: How did the place's melancholia impinge upon their teaching?

SD: I found that the love for the subject always lacked a dimension. I remember we used to know Book Nine of *The Aeneid* backwards because Father McGlinchey taught it to us so often. But never once until afterwards did it occur to me that *The Aeneid* is a great, powerful piece of political propaganda; and that if you don't see it as a political poem, you're not seeing it in any full sense at all. This is something that you find in colonised societies: a turn towards the aesthetic and away from the political is the consequence of people who become successful at study, at writing. And then the idea that the aesthetic and the political are connected becomes the position of an extremist. I'm saying this sundering between the political and the aesthetic is in fact the product of an education that depends on domination. The easy transference of the habits of adoration from religious to secular things, so characteristic of a consumer society, was already done for us in a premonitory way by teaching us the autonomy of art and the adoration that goes with its transcendence. The word for that, in Benjamin and Adorno, is 'phantasmagoria'; but I was some time and distance removed from that perception and concept.

A civilised teacher asked you to appreciate the complexity and the beauty of the text that you were dealing with. Once you got that kind of appreciation grown in you, even in a hothouse way, all the other stuff was regarded as lesser than that, junior to it, the perversion of it. I used to wonder, if I stay with this will I become a person of the book. The path that opened then was that of teaching. The people who are people of the book were now people who were interested in aesthetic and historical things of great complexity. All those beatings were elements of an unfortunate doctrinaire or ideological warp. The way the Catholic Church talks about sexuality, the way the British or US governments talk about democracy: you know that each of them has a scandalous record in precisely those areas that they're most eager to defend themselves in, and that both of them are actually disqualified to say anything persuasive about human sexuality or democratic regimes and processes. But that's precisely the kind of shift I'm talking about. It's safe to stay in the 'historical', as long as that is bookish. It has nothing to do with the harsh world of the beatings, whether they're beatings by the police or beatings by priests. The coercion, the brainwashing, the sexual disturbance of the priests, the endless political provocations of the police – these are things that are transient. But when you're dealing with Wordsworth's poetry, you're dealing with something enduring and permanent. That pup was sold to us over and over again. Still is being sold. Ordinary people live real lives and scholars live illusory lives. The whole point is that there is a separation between the two. You can never in this society legitimately talk about writing really in the glare of the real life, because if you do so, you're being an ideologue.

MF: When did the changes you saw growing in the North begin to manifest themselves?

SD: Here in the Northern Ireland of 1951, the beating of that little girl by the RUC man; October 1968 is another critical year when changes began to make themselves manifest. But I also think of the year 1972, not just because it's the Bloody Sunday year, not just because of the proroguing of Stormont, but because that's the big year of assassination. Many of the assassinations we'll never know the full truth about, but many of them were carried out by security forces, so-called. But the other point about 1972 is it's also the first year in two hundred years that British manufacturing showed a deficit in export. It's the beginning of Thatcherite Britain. It's the beginning of a Britain where the financial system takes precedence over the manufacturing system. What we were seeing in Northern Ireland was the old colonial behaviour – murder and oppression and all the rest of it – under various forms of disguise. But we were actually looking at a state that was beginning to lose the capacity to keep on reproducing that colonial system. The city, so to say, overcame the mainland. Westminster was more important than Birmingham and Manchester. Britain lost its manufacturing precedence, I mean thoroughly. The rust belt started coming, and Northern Ireland was full of rust belts. There was that hiatus between the death of all those old industries and the new technologies which were really only to flower in the 1990s. So there's a whole period when the British State, the Irish State, actually have no secure economic foundation. The violence in a place like Northern Ireland is like an overhang from earlier periods. But there's no longer the capacity or the conditions for that state to survive as it has. Very often you saw things hanging on, surviving, after the conditions for their survival had disappeared. I always had this sense of the archaic. What used to be an up-to-date colonial system suddenly becomes archaic. Great Britain becomes a financial centre and then, as is now the case, when the financial system is threatened, there is no fallback position in manufacturing. This island keeps getting the reverberations from that. Generations brought up in one system very often hang on to the values of that system long after the conditions for the preservation of those values have begun to disappear. You can't manufacture a spontaneous response. So people then tended to very often look for some kind of alternative to the world of work, or of no work; the world of capitalism, to which Catholicism, we had heard, was allergic. The arts were the alternative. Sometimes it was music. Sometimes literature. It's strange how Catholics were more interested for a while in the arts than Protestants. Protestants didn't need that interest because they had jobs and didn't feel the need for education to the same extent as Catholics did.

MF: Is that sectarian divide still with us?

SD: The sectarian divide will be a permanent part of Northern Ireland as long as Northern Ireland exists. It can't but be: it's about the only form of stimulus the place has, but it's a stimulus that's decreasingly effective. Decreasingly effective and increasingly important for the place to survive. It had become in St. Columb's, socially and politically, increasingly important that this education should be got; and Catholicism as such was becoming decreasingly important as this education became increasingly so. When I began to understand this I sometimes got a sort of feeling of unreality, walking the corridors here as if I were inside out or as if I were walking in reverse or something. The place

actually was upside down, in a profound way. Education was going to break the unionists' hold, yes, but was also going to break the Catholic hold. And the unionists had to accept the Education Act because they were unionists and because it came from London. The Catholics had to accept the challenge of breaking unionism through education, but they thought education could remain Catholic whereas in fact it was the beginning of the end for Catholicism. You were walking into this vortex where things your parents thought were almost part of nature were revealing themselves as historical energies, historical institutions. They were actually flying past you. They were breaking up, even as you walked forward – but you didn't know into what. It was inevitable that it would be a vortex of violence. I think I'm speaking for a number of people in saying this: why has Northern Ireland always felt out of date? The bombing campaign, the obvious corruption of the judiciary, all of these things were being exposed too late. It was after they had died that you saw what they looked like.

All Northern Ireland has now is a kind of technological know-how, a Scandinavian solution to communal strife, which everybody knows is makeshift. The capacity for any group in Ireland to stimulate the kind of assent, consent, that actually gives authority its meaning is not there. You get all this consensual drivel about trauma and moving on and closure. That's just a society babbling into incoherence. Everything is now perfectly incoherent. Everybody can learn a little speech that's psychobabble with the American impulse to heighten it: you can be everything you want to be, all those idiotic and dangerous notions. That's a sign of the atomisation of a social system. What happens when the great institutions collapse: unionism, Catholicism, the broad collapse of communism, the death of twentieth century capitalism. This is all raining down past us now. This is when I feel it's like being back in St. Columb's. It's the same sensation that everything is flying past you. You think everything is inverted, and everybody is trying to say this is where authority lies. Disoriented people seem to be eccentric, drug addicts and drunkards, violent. To those who say violence is an aberration, I ask can you remember anywhere, anytime, when violence was not an integral part of a social or a political system? Violence is obviously part of an economic system like capitalism. Part of the problem in relation to St. Columb's was to say that violence was a strange aberration. It has become routine for people who'd been through here to object to the violence that they suffered at the hands of various teachers. It wasn't because Father Tierney drinks twenty-five whiskeys at night. It actually was a revelation to us (and we were idiots not to have realised it) that this was native to the system.

MF: And violence in the streets was also routine?

SD: It's equally the case that there was a lot of street violence, and a lot of that street violence was a reaction against specific people. I remember a man from a street nearby, Nelson Street, who was gay (I wouldn't have known the word then, I wouldn't have known the concept). And this man was abused in every possible way, so much so that he became the best stone-thrower in the district as a form of defence. He could split you open at twenty, thirty yards, no problem. I can't imagine the solitude of the life that he led there, behind the virtuoso of stone-throwing. Jehovah's Witnesses got no sympathy at all. I remember when they came round the doors, they were stoned out of the neighbourhood. I mean, a hailstorm of rocks. There were regular fights between the top section and the bottom section of the street I lived in, between the other streets in the area, between the Protestants in the Fountain and ourselves. Sunday morning was a favourite time to launch Napoleonic assaults on the nearest enemy neighbourhood because you could keep at it all day then. You didn't have to go to school. That kind of world had been deformed, broken, in various ways. It's one of the standard laments, isn't it, of the auld decency school of sociology that you don't have as many interesting characters as there used to be around. By which they mean people who had been wrecked, mentally wrecked, broken down, were walking round the streets talking to themselves or in some state of decrepitude that was taken as entertainment for others. The high incidence of such unfortunates was a mark of what Derry was like. When you came to this school and you saw the marked incidence of very eccentric people among the teachers, you were joining up the dots in a way, and saying there is some kind of connection here. All this eccentricity, but what is the connection?

There's an old story about the great Frantz Fanon when he was in Morocco. He was a psychiatrist, and one of the stories about him took place during the Algerian war of independence from France. He was put in charge of a hospital for people who were incurably mentally ill. There were sixty people in the particular hospital. He found that all sixty of them were manacled to the wall, in straitjackets. So the first thing he did was have the manacles and the straitjackets removed. He worked for several years with these people and formed a football team with them.

It sounds a bit like an American movie. The idea was this is the kind of education, this is the kind of heroic teacher/doctor/priest who takes a community out of its shackles, and out of its madness, and makes it healthy again. The only problem with the story is that after a few years he gave up and went and joined the FLN to fight the French because he felt the violence that had created those people was too great to be outfaced by some form of therapy. Therapy was only useful in completely restructured situations. I think now we're in a sort of similar situation. Therapy only extends structural injustices.

MF: In the context of these structural injustices, how do you see October 5th, 1968?

SD: The violent nature of the state was not just revealed, but, for once, televised. The place became scandalous. The assumption was that when the scandal of the violence is exposed on television, then in some way that will help fix the violence. In fact it only intensified it. The violence was traded between various groupings then. The people who began the violence against the civil rights demonstrators then became the defenders of the status quo. You got the usual hypocrisies and passing the buck about where violence lies. There was a possibility or there seemed to be a possibility in '68 that there would be some kind of emancipatory result. We haven't seen it yet; '68 was quickly followed by '72, and then that long spiral down into the first ceasefire [1994], and all the Elastoplast operation that's gone on since then. Change has not reached the point where people can find a form of violence that they can accept as legitimate. You've got to legitimise violence in a society in order to believe that you live in a peaceful society. There's no legitimate violence in a state like Northern Ireland; there are only forms of violence that are hypocritically pursued, but don't have the consent of the people. That's why the Republic is a nation state that says that we live in this state which has a monopoly of violence. There are problems with that too, but essentially that's a stabilising feature. Up here violence was never legitimised in the same way. It wasn't assented to that there was a monopoly of violence on any side. As a consequence the place was always all liable to rupture. The kinds of violence that were carried on from street level right up to the level of the army and the police had an element of the arbitrary to them because they weren't disciplined by legitimacy. It became often more and more arbitrary, and disturbing and vindictive, ending in torture victims.

MF: Yesterday, in the car, you mentioned Toynbee, the British historian, who had a theory about education acts. Could you talk about that in relation to Northern Ireland from 1947 through to 1968?

SD: This notion was, to my knowledge, first put out by Arnold Toynbee in one of his multi-volume histories, in which he said, taking the 1870 Education Act as an example, to see the consequences of an important education act you have to take the date in which it is passed and then add twenty years.

His shtick then was to say the Education Act of 1870 in Britain produced mass literacy. Its effect was 1890/91: the yellow press, the *Daily Mail*. People are now literate but they're not cultured – rather the reverse, according to Toynbee. We've now managed to get literacy without culture, and so this is the high culture/low culture divide that we've been plagued by since. And in some ways you could do the same simple sociological arithmetic with Northern Ireland. So 1947, add twenty/twenty-one years to get 1968. Then the Education Act has made that difference that has challenged the state of the minority which was previously effectively downtrodden. It found through education a way to make their voice heard. And the state was so cast iron and so

profoundly stupid in its repressive measures that it couldn't ever be flexible enough to accommodate even the mildest of demands without exhibiting violence. As a consequence, that state managed to sign its own death warrant. So you could say '47, '68, '72. There's a sequence there. But the new situation in 1972 is in fact the old situation. It's British rule in Northern Ireland without the official help of the unionists. It's a design for political constipation which is the only form of emancipation possible for this place. The reality is direct rule. It's a situation that can't be solved internally for this place. The whole colonial relation itself must be dissolved before there's a solution.

Eamonn McCann

What comes through strongest in McCann's interview is his involvement in all aspects of the Bogside where he grew up and continues to live. Independent institutions defined the Bogside of his early youth: St. Vincent de Paul, the Credit Union. The Bogside was very independent from the rest of society. It had its own culture. Showbands with tubas and pipes played. The Wolfe Tone band was popular. There were dozens of football teams: every street seemed to have one. Sometimes a league would be played out between a handful of streets.

Politics was popular too. Although McCann grew up in a tiny house – two rooms upstairs, two down – the front parlour was hardly ever used except for labour relations meetings. Though his dad did not smoke, the rest did and smoke would emerge from the room as the men debated politics. He seemed to inhale his politics at a very tender age. Some of McCann's earliest emotions included a sense of indignation that Catholics didn't have jobs in the Guildhall. That was utterly intolerable. The church's domination was absolute in the Derry of his youth. They followed rituals that young Catholics today would scarcely be aware of: the nine first Fridays and the five first Saturdays. 'The church was your whole life.' It was in this atmosphere of sport, politics, music, community organisations and (underpinning everything) the church that the socialist thinker, McCann, grew up.

McCann refers to his native area as one of 'a number of green islands in the midst of the orange sea'. In his political assessment of Northern Ireland, he reflects Deane, who used similar imagery to characterise the North. 'Sociologically, one might describe the place as an archipelago of submerged psychic islands separated and inundated by currents of hatred, ignorance and mistrust.' ('Mugwumps and Reptiles', *Atlantis*, 1972).

McCann's analysis in this interview condemns the benighted
unionist administration and how
unprepared it was for the Bogside,
once it benefited from education
and was led by people who would
no longer tolerate the *ancien régime*.
The Bogside was populous. It had an
abundance of youth and a tightly-
knit community which lent itself to
banding together against the prevalent political structure.

People of different hues of political persuasion could play together
in concerts, on the football pitch (though not the GAA pitch because of
the GAA's own rules) and on the boards. Many people, including Daly,
believed that players from both communities acting on stage together
could meld the torn political situation.

I met a Catholic Derry man who was invited to an Orange Order meeting in Derry. At the end of the meeting, everyone sang 'God
Save the Queen'. Later a man approached him and said that he hoped
the singing of the anthem had not made him feel uncomfortable. The
Catholic replied, 'I was not offended, but I was disappointed. You did
not play the third verse and you did not let me sing the anthem in Irish.'
Wee Willie Doherty also seemed to have contrived a way to accommodate implacably opposed traditions. Interviewing McCann, just before
he told the story about Wee Willie Doherty who 'could play "Kevin
Barry" and "The Sash"', McCann pointed his finger directly at me. It is
typical of Derry to point when the punchline comes.

St. Patrick's Day, 1951, is a key date in the coming of age of the
'Eleven Plus Generation'. Coincidentally, McCann's first experience of a
riot was at that same St. Patrick's Day Parade, 1951. McCann was eight
years old or so. Followers of the Nationalist Party were baton-charged
on Shipquay Street. He did not feel that Catholics were being put in
their place at all. Being very young, he ended up stealing fruit out of
Colt's Shop (Fresh Fruit, Flowers Daily) on Sackville Street. The young
rioters ran up Sackville Street, retreated back, paused to re-arm with
stones and stormed up the street once more. It was great fun. The photo

of little Helen Kellaigh, the six year old girl with blond hair from Great James Street, getting batoned was subsequently printed in the *Derry Journal*. A rhyme of the day encapsulated the event:

'Inside the walls
There were some squalls
No Tricolour inside the walls.'

Like John Hume, McCann went to Rosemount primary school, one of the many primary schools in the area. He passed the Eleven Plus and won a scholarship to go to St. Columb's – the best school for a Catholic boy like him. It turns out that the young McCann was a natural examinee: 'I was a good bullshitter. Even if I knew only one thing, I could expand upon it. I could adapt the question to suit what I knew.' McCann never encountered pressure from his parents to go into any particular profession. When the envelope notifying him of his Eleven Plus success arrived, his mother was ecstatic:

'She kissed me and hugged me. I can only remember one other time in her life when she was so happy. It was the Grand National – the only race of the year in which our house backed a horse. She asked me to pick a winner and I zoomed in with a pen nib on a horse called Russian Hero. Against huge odds, sixty-one to one, it romped home first in the 1949 Grand National.'

McCann's first day at St. Columb's left quite an impression on him. Father McFeely intoned that those boys who did not want to become priests were to become 'the leaders of the Catholic people'. McCann remembers resenting this duty. In 1954, when McCann entered St. Columb's, there were six classes of new entrants: 2A, 2B, 2C, 2D, 2E and 2F. Another encounter on that momentous first day involved Eddie Mahon, former goalkeeper for Derry City, who recalls that McCann evinced a leaning toward the priesthood from an early age. On their first day in St. Columb's boys had to choose between Ancient Greek and French as subjects of study. Mahon writes:

'I shared a desk (for alphabetical reasons, 'M' and 'Mc') with a certain Eamonn McCann on that fateful day. And as the president, Fr McFeely (later to be Bishop McFeely of Raphoe) made his way round the senior study, he arrived first with the redoubtable McCann. "French or Greek, McCann?" enquired the president. "If you want to be a priest which do you do?" queried McCann. "You do Greek, McCann!" "I'll do Greek, then, Father," said the future member of the Socialist Party' (*Seeking the Kingdom*, p. 100).

Eddie Mahon became the only Ancient Greek-speaking goalkeeper in the League of Ireland and he blames this on McCann. They have remained lifelong friends and attend every fixture at the Brandywell together. 'The thing about old school pals,' he told me, 'is that you cannot deceive them.' (*Is maith an scáthán súil charad*/A true friend's eye is a good mirror). Goalkeepers were regarded with contempt in St. Columb's. Usually ten people would be picked for a football game. Then the goalkeeper would be picked. McCann's footballing Achilles tendon has been recorded earlier, but he was good at handball – which, alas, counted for little in St. Columb's. Deane was also a star footballer, poetry in motion, according to McCann. He had great timing. He could have easily been a professional player. City boys played soccer on a gravelly pitch at the college. Boarders tended to play GAA football. Eddie Mahon was a boarder who – against the tide – played soccer. He was very bright and he liked St. Columb's. He was popular there and it is said that he cried on his last day at St. Columb's. He is a defender of McCann's footballing efforts. Others are less charitable: 'McCann couldn't kick snow off a rope. He was like a rag-doll when the ball came near him.' St. Columb's' sportsday was held in The Brandywell. For many boys this escape from the college grounds was a timeless moment – after a race they would eat chocolate and drink minerals with friends.

At school McCann once played the fiddle, but music at St. Columb's was also subject to the eccentricity of some teachers. Father McFeely once stopped a jazz concert because a boy was swinging his hips and singing '*C'est Ci Bon*' which Father McFeely denounced as '*le jazz Americain*', so obnoxious to him were the boy's pelvic pulsations. A French teacher at this time was known as 'Corkey' because he was an alcoholic. He was also known as '*Dicté*' because all he did by way of teaching was to dictate texts.

Occasionally students would counter this eccentricity and attitudinising with pranks. A teacher once flew off the handle and clattered a boy. The boy rolled on the floor shouting, 'My eye, my eye'. The teacher momentarily believed that he had taken the boy's eye out. St. Columb's was a disquieting place to be and students had to learn survival.

On another occasion, McCann spent a class undermining a brutal Irish teacher. By the very end of the class, before leaving for his cigarette, the priest made a burst for McCann. McCann secreted himself so deftly underneath his desk that no matter where the priest aimed his boot or however he swung his fists, he could not successfully land a blow. When the priest finally relented and left the room, McCann emerged from below and said, 'If he had hit me, I would have killed him'. His classmates fell around the room laughing.

McCann's maths teacher, whose nickname was 'The Bird', once walked into class and saw that a boy had scribbled on the blackboard:

'Hail to thee, blithe spirit!
Bird thou never wert.'

McCann exclaimed, 'It is Shelley'. Even though McCann hadn't scribbled it, and though he had correctly identified the poet (it is Shelley's 'Ode to a Skylark'), 'The Bird' nonetheless took him outside and 'beat the shite' out of him.

The Senior Study was also used for detention. McCann would arrive into the Senior Study after being thrown out of class – chewing gum, with a bundle of books under his arm, uncombed curly hair and unshaven locks. Younger boys looked up to him. At the age of fourteen or fifteen, McCann started to speak at public debates in the Columcille Club. Older men were amazed at the talent he evinced as a debater and encouraged him all the way. Younger students were inspired by his bravery in public speaking. Famously, McCann, when still a student at St. Columb's, debated with Brian Faulkner (the rabid unionist who introduced internment without trial) on TV. During the debate, McCann had the politician backpedaling. Back in St. Columb's, some priests wondered had they really seen 'this display of arrogance' from McCann. Priests knew that McCann had a following and they disliked it. St. Columb's defined itself as a junior seminary. It wasn't really a bulwark against unionist domination, as McCann sees it.

On the podium McCann fires out words like the thud of racehorse hooves on turf. He has the mien of a dervish and entertains like a box-

ing tout. 'We raised a generation of kamikaze teenagers whose sport it would be to hurtle down Rossville Street with stones in their hands to take on the British Army on a Saturday afternoon.' When I mentioned McCann's debating prowess to Coulter, who was also known as a debater in Derry, he agreed and thought that McCann should have been a QC. (McCann acknowledged that he wouldn't have minded the money.) Coulter's comments on McCann's rhetorical verve come later in this book. McCann has remained his own man politically – neither Sinn Féin nor SDLP – throughout the Troubles.

McCann is another past pupil who was hugely influenced by S.B. O'Kelly. O'Kelly would tell the boys that 'books are the only thing that makes life worth living'. It must have pleased him to see that several of his students became writers. He confided to a student who returned to visit him, 'all my pupils have surpassed me years ago'. (It was Leonardo da Vinci's belief that the only duty pupils owe their masters is to surpass them.) S.B. O'Kelly, also known as 'Squeak', said that McCann 'made my life a misery'. There were only six pupils in the upper English class. Once, when S.B. O'Kelly spoke of Henry James, McCann pretended for twenty minutes that O'Kelly was talking about a famous jazzman of the day. Some of the staff actually liked him. McCann was very bright. He had piercing blue eyes and he was fun. Once there was an All-Derry essay competition during McCann's time at St. Columb's, open to all schools. S.B. O'Kelly's remit was to enter only two essays, but he had three star essayists in his class – Jude Collins, McCann and a boy named Dicky. S.B. O'Kelly refused to tell the boys which two of the three essays he submitted. But the fact became obvious when Dicky took second prize and McCann took first. S.B. O'Kelly was mortified that Jude Collins found out in this way that he had been sidelined. (Collins felt honoured that O'Kelly cared.) Everyone was proud of McCann for having won the competition. S.B. O'Kelly is on record as saying that of all the students he had ever had, McCann had the most wondrous mind. He would have written any of his contemporaries into a cocked hat.

McCann is sorry that he did not listen more to their revered English teacher. He wishes he had taken English Literature in Queen's instead of 'boring psychology'. If he had done so, he thinks he might have spent less of his university time in the pub.

There was something sacred about the Irish language in St. Columb's and McCann was a gadfly to Irish teachers. One day when a certain priest was teaching Irish, McCann was characteristically being a lig (Derry: to be messing). The exercise was to render English names in the Irish language. Hugh became Aoghan, Peter became Peadar and so forth. The priest asked the boys for a name each. McCann asked what Percival is in Irish. McCann continued to goad him, asking what Cecil is in Irish. The priest's temples began to redden. What was distinctive about that particular priest's punishment was he actually used his fists. The priest stormed to McCann's desk and gave him a ferocious blow. The cut worm forgives the plow?

(I spoke to a St. Columb's boy who later became a teacher there. He told me that that priest was a wonderful colleague, in contrast to his ruthless approach to teaching. His father had been a TD, de Valera's henchman.)

St. Columb's was, however, not all fisticuffs. The boys once performed *Tones of Money*, a West End farce, as the school play. McCann played the female lead in drag. And one scene involved kissing Heaney. The choice of Christmas plays at St. Columb's was quite imperialist: Gilbert and Sullivan or Shakespeare.

There was complexity in the make-up of the staff. Once Father Keough caught Jude Collins reading *Vanity Fair* (novels were absolutely forbidden) in the study hall. He looked at the cover and smiled – then let him continue reading. The thaw in disciplining was already apparent. Day-boys were inclined to answer back, even to insult. They might even use sexual innuendos when talking to a priest. But if you provoked someone in authority, you got hammered. In a Religious Education class that was given by a young lay teacher, for example, McCann, in his senior year, pushed too far. McCann went to 'Borderland', the same dancehall that the teacher frequented. One day McCann asked him, 'Sir, did you enjoy Borderland last night?' The teacher 'beat the shit out of McCann, nearly murdered him'.

McCann had never been back to the Bishop Street school before the making of *The Boys of St. Columb's*. He wondered what impact visiting it would have. McCann imagined that it would be quite dramatic. Neither had Brady returned – who also anticipated an emotional and difficult reunion with the college. Curiosity brought McCann back. While filming in the chapel at St. Columb's, McCann was taken by how little the place had changed. 'It has been the same for two thousand years,' he ventured.

In the chapel, McCann also recalled how during retreat he once tried to overthrow a motion against Elvis Presley during Father Flanagan's homily on the grounds that it was unfair to deprecate 'The King' when he was not there to defend himself.

McCann had a crusading attitude towards those who valued respectability which grew during his time at Queen's. After getting elected to the editorial board of *Gown*, the student magazine at Queen's, the first headline during McCann's tenure there read, 'McCann lashes the VC' [Vice-Chancellor]. Still, there was not much sense of siege at Queen's. I spoke to a St. Columb's boy who was chairman of both the Cumann na Gaedheal and the GAA Club at Queen's. He remembers that these societies were treated fairly in the funding stakes. The only tension in Queen's was at The Hop on Saturday night after the last dance, when 'God Save the Queen' began to play. Prudent folk would exit quickly – or position themselves beside the door. On one occasion, not only did McCann refuse to stand for the British anthem, he got out in the middle of the floor and sat down – a prime target for a hiding. Only for the GAA men intervening on his behalf, he would surely have been beaten badly. On that occasion, his act of *lèse majesté* went unpunished. Another such act, less bold and pronounced, but the same in kind, was Heaney's semi-refusal to stand for the Queen's anthem at an Offenbach opera: Heaney joked in an interview that when he attended opera during his student days and the British national anthem played, he and his friends would semi-stand for it.

One former student likens McCann to the terrier that faces down a wild horse. Every society needs such citizens – fearless, without a thought of security for the future. McCann has constantly challenged people throughout his life. St. Columb's embodied the sense of rectitude of the establishment and with its utter complacency, assuredness of its place and need to continue. McCann attacked every shibboleth and tilted at every sacred cow. It is hard to over-emphasise how much a risk it was in the early sixties to lash the VC, as McCann did in Queen's. It was unprecedented. If McCann had not done it, it would not be as easy for the present generation to stake a claim on their rights and liberty today.

When I meet McCann for pre-interview he is ten minutes late. He looks at his watch to verify it before his complimentary pot of tea arrives at his local in Derry. He has a few phone calls to field from people he is representing for the trade union before our conversation gets going. He wants to avert a court case which would mean days of wrangling in Belfast. He bargains with the barristers who phone him up and eventually gets his deal. The most recent public legal entanglement he was involved in was a trespassing charge. Back at the beginning of Bush's war, McCann and a few wily cohorts occupied an armaments factory, Raytheon, in Derry. The trial (which ended in mid-June 2008) was pending and there was a real risk that he would be in jail when we started shooting the film. Someone quipped that we should film him on the inside. This is where St. Columb's boys end up? McCann seems entirely unperturbed by the prospect of jail. He has got this far in life without having to spend in excess of a week at a time under Her Majesty's Service. He faced the prospect of serving up to six weeks' jail time on this occasion. But that was six weeks away from the mobile phone and his rackety life in Derry to catch up on his reading. He represented himself, as ever. Advocacy is his middle name. Thankfully, the jury's verdict ruled on the side of those who had protested.

McCann stood on the steps outside the Belfast's Laganside Court (11 June 2008) and said: 'We have not denied or apologised for what we did at the Raytheon plant in summer of 2006. All of us believe it was the best thing we ever did in our lives'.

Sitting in a bar in Water Street, the border is three miles to the west, three miles to the north and also three miles to the south. Only the eastern vista faces into Northern Ireland. Thus Derry is surrounded by the protective buffer of the Republic. The city may be an Orange mecca, but it has always been assured of its green identity too. From the age of twelve or so, McCann would cycle to Fadden in Donegal to swim. He would smuggle butter and cigarettes on his way back. But – unlike Deane, say – McCann never felt the least bit more free when across the border. He never shared that patriotic sentiment. As Deane remembered:

'You could get eggs, you could get all sorts of things that were rationed in the North. It was nice to be able to walk over the border and back. It was a strange feeling, going over a little humpback bridge. You know, over here: the North. Over here: the Free State. And that name, the Free State, stuck with it. I liked the name itself, and the memory of Sunday walks crossing the border' (*Journal of Irish Studies,* Japan, 2007).

McCann, on the other hand, 'never had a patriotic sentiment in my life'. He identified far more with The Undertones whose ambition – regardless of what was happening in Northern Ireland during the 1980s – was to have a hit on Top of the Pops. To fly by the nets of patriotism is an essential element of McCann's socialist ethic. Nonetheless, there is something in the Northern Irish condition that almost insists that every aspect of life adhere to part of a historical narrative. History is almost inescapable. The Undertones wrote, 'It's gonna happen, happens all the time ... till you change your mind', and sang that lyric on Top of the Pops on the night before Bobby Sands died. Its coded message warned the British authorities that they must relent.

McCann remembers the many poems by Hopkins which he learned by heart at St. Columb's. Hopkins, a convert to Catholicism, was trapped by rigid Catholicism, entrapped within his church. He resided in Newman House. McCann quotes:

The Caged Skylark (1882)

'As a dare-gale skylark scanted in a dull cage
Man's mounting spirit in his bone-house, mean house, dwells
...
That bird beyond the remembering his free fells;
This in drudgery, day-labouring-out life's age.

Man's spirit will be flesh-bound when found at best,
But uncumbered: meadow-down is not distressed
For a rainbow footing it nor he for his bones risen.'

After Queen's, McCann went to London and did a variety of jobs – labouring, mainly – before he settled on a job as an arborculturist, transplanting and pruning trees. He and his cockney co-workers loaded into a van at 5.00 am and sang Blake's 'Jerusalem' on the way to work.

'And did those feet in ancient time
Walk upon England's mountains green?
And was the holy Lamb of God
On England's pleasant pastures seen?

I will not cease from mental fight,
Nor shall my sword sleep in my hand,
Till we have built Jerusalem,
In England's green and pleasant land.'

In 1968, home from London to visit his younger sister, McCann's old friend Dermie O'Clenaghan asked him if he would help to block a road with a car in protest against poor housing. McCann agreed and gradually became involved in the civil rights movement.

McCann may be seen as the fallen angel of St. Columb's. His negative feelings are apparent in this interview. But his contribution to this history is undeniable, just as he would not deny the element of self-definition he received through his education at St. Columb's. When Martin O'Neill gave a scathing speech on becoming an Alumnus of St. Columb's – in 2002, soon after he became manager of Celtic Football Club – naming the brutal priests, McCann was not present, but he did contact

VOTE McCANN LABOUR

O'Neill about it the following day to get the text of the speech to use for one of his columns. Alas, the speech had been off the cuff and Mc-Cann did not have material for a column. But that does not take from the column. It is an opinion, shared by a few, that McCann's columns have been among the best in Irish journalism over the past half century. His has been an individual yet Northern voice. When I researched this film and book, I learned a lot from McCann's writings.

MF: Can you describe the area in which you grew up?

EM: The Bogside I grew up in was a very oppressed place, but it could also be a very oppressive place. Very tight knit community. Obviously it had a feeling of embattlement about it. It was just teeming with people and teeming with children in particular. My memory of the Bogside is of streets absolutely crowded with children playing everything from football to spinning tops to conkers and anything else that was going. I can see now, looking back, that the Bogside had a particularly distinct sense of itself and people from the Bogside were very well aware that they came from a particular community and that that community fitted into, or didn't fit into, the surrounding political and social circumstances of Northern Ireland. The church dominated almost all the social life of the Bogside. We weren't aware of poverty at the time because we didn't know anything different. Appalling housing conditions, looking back. My house had an attic. I used to sleep under the slates, you know, which was wonderful because you could actually stand on a chair and poke your head out the skylight.

MF: How was it culturally?

EM: There was a lot of cultural life in the Bogside. Many little tin huts or halls. I can remember brilliant concerts going on just for local people by local people. Wee Willie Doherty, who could play two tunes on the tin whistle, two whistles out of each side of his mouth. He could play 'Kevin Barry' and 'The Sash' simultaneously, a very non-sectarian whistler was Willie. An awful lot of musical talent came out of the Bog-side, usually pipe bands and flute bands and brass bands. We had half a dozen showbands running from the Bogside alone. It was a pastime, a form of self-expression and so on.

MF: Is it fair to say it was politically well-informed and conscious of its status within the city?

EM: There were a lot of well educated people in the Bogside – and I don't mean this in a patronising way – but people taught themselves. People were quite well read. And in my memory, we had a great interest in foreign affairs. For example, I remember Cyprus and Archbishop Makarios. And there were heated arguments going on in the street about Cyprus and about Iran in 1953, the overthrow of Dr Masadiq by the CIA. I remember a woman across the street saying one day that the Shah was the rightful ruler of Iran. And my father came storming across the street, saying 'rightful ruler, my God!' and stormed into the house. You don't get that very much these days. It had a sense of the wider world which perhaps we don't have today.

Everybody knew that the things that were suffered in the Bogside – deprivation and poverty and lack of opportunity – had to do with the fact that we were Catholics. Because we were Catholics, none of us would ever work in the Guildhall, we thought. We'd never have fair play in employment (although my father was usually in work). We would never get a house in the Waterside or in the North Ward where houses were being built. The Bogside was just bulging with people. I mean, we had a population pyramid like that of Britain in the middle of the nineteenth century, not in the middle of the twentieth century.

People used to say that eventually Catholics would outbreed Protestants and then we'd have a United Ireland and then everything would be OK. Or the Protestants would one day wake up and realise they were Irish after all, and the North of Ireland would disappear. There was always a tiny minority who thought we just have to fight them for it: only the gun would ever change these things.

And it just seemed that that's the way things were going to be. We were one of a number of little green islands in the midst of the orange sea.

MF: So the Eleven Plus came in with the 1947 Education Act. What impact did it make?

EM: The Eleven Plus, when it came in, was regarded as a route out of the Bogside. Individuals would be able to escape from their environment through education. There was always a great emphasis on education. It was sort of an educational obstacle course. You had to pass exams. But if you did pass them, you could go on and then go to secondary school and go on to university. I can remember a chap called Paddy Doherty who was the first person from our street to go to university. The area was almost agog that somebody from the Bogside was able to go to university because that was something that middle class Catholics would do. You could be educated to escape entirely from the constrictions of the Bogside. That only came in with the Eleven Plus. People waited on tenterhooks for the results and there were great celebrations. I remember when I got the letter that said I passed the Eleven Plus. Then I remember my mother rushing across and kissing me. It was a Saturday morning when the letter came. We were the first generation to have this opportunity. It was made clear to you, from the very beginning, at the age of eleven, that a great deal was expected of you. We were warned at the age of eleven, 'you must not waste this'.

MF: Another initiative (apart from education) of the welfare state, brought in by the Attlee Government, was to institute free health care.

Your father was a staunch socialist, so surely that aspect of
post-war legislation was also
welcomed in your house?

EM: The National Health
Service meant an awful lot in
an area like the Bogside. Free
medical treatment, free orange
juice, free malt – I mean malt
was lovely, healthy too. I used
to eat big tablespoonfuls. My
father's great hero, the biggest
hero of his life, was Aneurin
Bevan, the Minister for Health
in the post-war Labour government who introduced the National Health Service. And one
of the first phrases I knew in
politics was 'Tories are vermin'.
Aneurin Bevan said that in the

Commons when the Conservative Party opposed the Health Service.
He spat that at them across the dispatch box.

MF: How did you find St. Columb's when you first went there?

EM: I didn't regard St. Columb's, when I was going up there for the
first time, as an alien place. But it certainly was a place that was not for
me.

I remember my very first day, very first class in St. Columb's, being
in the class that was just off the senior corridor. Day one. My first introduction to class and there was this priest (I won't mention his name)
from rural south Derry. He was going round asking people, 'where do
you come from?' And he came to me and said, 'where do you come
from McCann?' I said, 'I come from Rossville Street,' and he immediately shot back, 'Rossville Street? That's where you wash once a month!'
And that was letting me know. At eleven years of age. He was letting me
know what my station was and letting me know that he didn't believe

it was appropriate that the likes of me from Rossville Street should be there at all. Interlopers. I was an interloper. And it is well chronicled how a generation of intelligent and articulate and sometimes belligerent young Catholics came on to the scene in Northern Ireland; and the way that that impacted on and disturbed the unionist consensus in Northern Ireland. But it is not as frequently recognised that the Eleven Plus, and the fact that people from the Bogside were going into secondary education, had something of a shuddering effect on the Catholic middle classes as well. They saw the great unwashed sort of invading the territory that had been the property of lawyers and the others who lived in leafy places like Marlborough Street.

MF: How would you describe the ethos of St. Columb's?

EM: The purpose of St. Columb's was to produce priests. Father McFeely, the President of St. Columb's, said to us, 'this isn't a school, this is a junior seminary'. And he explained to us that the function of St. Columb's was to keep the church going by supplying a constant stream of priests. And its secondary function was to replenish the Catholic professional classes who would dominate the entire Catholic community and ensure that the Catholic community was kept safe for Catholicism and the Catholic faith.

I think that one of the reasons why people like me had an abrasive relationship with St. Columb's eventually is of course that people from Rossville Street and the Bogside who came into St. Columb's had a different attitude to the one that was held by St. Columb's – as a sort of corporate entity held by the church. We were a bit wilder. We were soccer people, not Gaelic football people.

There was that clash between the outlook and the assumptions that people who came from the Bogside had on the one hand, and the assumptions that St. Columb's had about itself.

MF: Did you know many of the other participants in this film at school?

EM: I knew Seamus Heaney. Seamus Heaney was the Head Prefect. I knew Seamus Deane because Seamus Deane's father was a close friend of my own father and so I knew him through that. And I knew the

Deane family. They lived a bit above us, up from Rossville street. I knew Gerry and Eamon.

Phil Coulter I knew very well. Phil was in the same class as I was. He was into music even in those days. Always on about music. I think he wanted to become a classical musician. Wasn't he lucky that didn't work out?

MF: How do you view St. Columb's now?

EM: I think when we all look back on our schooldays and so on we filter out the bad bits. But really I hated going into St. Columb's most mornings. There was an element of fear in St. Columb's, too, by contemporary standards.

The regime at St. Columb's was quite brutal and was run by fear. It was run by a lot of brutality – not just slaps, but the use of fists. I was knocked unconscious in an Irish class once for something very, very trivial. The teacher hit me flush in the face with his fist. He wouldn't get away with that now. There were very large priests, big men, over six feet. There was capricious punishment for nothing at all. They would come in and say, 'Kerry, think of a number'. Kerry at the back of the class would say two. Ok, Patton, one. McLucas, two. Come out here, McLucas. He would beat him around the class and then say, 'don't blame me, blame Kerry, he picked your number'.

Some of the punishments that they had were bizarre and sadistic. I remember being made to kneel on the floor and take my toes, keep them up off the ground with my hands out in the front of me, so that my balance was in the fulcrum of the knees. And the teacher said, 'open your mouth', and he put a chalk duster into my mouth and then would invite me to nod my head and agree that I was a waster, a scoundrel, a no good who should be out digging ditches and not here in St. Columb's wasting teachers' times. When I look back on it now, I ask myself what the hell was going on in that guy's mind. What sort of shape is that guy's personality in to behave like that? I'm sure there were minds warped by their experiences in St. Columb's.

Looking back on it, I think some of the priests were clinically insane, I really do. And they were obviously very frustrated people. I understand them better now and indeed have met certain priests in subse-

quent years. I got to talk to them and realised that these were lonely people; some of them had become priests just because their parents had pushed them into it or they couldn't think of anything else to do. Or it was an approved career path if you were a young Catholic. What a narrow life to have. I look back now and I feel sorry for some of the priests, I genuinely do.

MF: Can you describe what happened on October 5th, 1968?

EM: The seeds of the October 5th march in Derry lay not in nationalist agitation or agitation against the Orange state, but in housing and unemployment campaigns that had been going on in Derry. The Labour Party was the strongest political element involved. The Nationalist Party originally saw the agitation of the civil rights movement as a challenge to itself. I was one of a number of people – six, eight, ten of us – who decided to carry the agitation onto a different dimension which became marching on the street. My expectation was that the civil rights movement was going to transcend the sectarian division. It was going to put an end to sectarian politics in Northern Ireland by shifting the axis of political debate in Derry to, in broad terms, a class dimension. Of course, that's not the way it worked out.

You can trace a direct line from October 1968 through to Bloody Sunday. What made October 5th the phenomenon that it became was not the march itself or the intention of the marchers. It actually was the reaction of the state, in the form of the RUC, to the march. Once the march was assaulted by the RUC, it seemed that sooner or later this was going to become a fight against the state. But that wasn't clear at the time. At least it wasn't clear to me.

MF: Did the coming of age of those who had benefited from the 1947 Education Act make October 5th happen?

EM: The fact that there was a generation of Catholics who had gone to secondary school as a result of the Eleven Plus examination certainly was a material factor in the development of the civil rights movement – there was a self-confidence. If you had been to St. Columb's and you went to Queen's University and you came back to Derry you were less likely to placidly accept being treated as a second class citizen. You'd been to England working, you were mixing with students, you came back and these deadheads who ran the Unionist Party in Derry were still trying to treat you like dirt. There were also changes in the wider world. There were economic changes, more educated politics generally.

MF: What are your memories of Bloody Sunday?

EM: There have been incidents in which more people were killed in Northern Ireland than on Bloody Sunday. Just the month previous to Bloody Sunday, there were fifteen people killed at the McGurk's Bar bombing. There were other comparable massacres in terms of the human toll. But Bloody Sunday was an assault by the state. It doesn't fit into the Orange/Green template. That's what makes it distinctive. Bloody Sunday was not an atrocity committed by one community against another. It was compounded by the fact that just eleven weeks later, the Lord Chief Justice of England, the highest legal authority in the land, the custodian of constitutional rectitude, came into our midst and pronounced that really no offence had been committed on Bloody Sunday. In effect, he said that the people there deserved it. Lord Widgery said that explicitly: that if the people hadn't been marching, they wouldn't have been massacred. Which, as a statement of fact, that's fair enough.

But, gosh, as a moral statement it leaves everything to be desired. The highest legal authority in these islands, the British authority, had come in and exonerated the soldiers. To suggest to people after that that they should seek redress for their problems through constitutional means was just laughable.

Bloody Sunday was the definitive moment when the real trouble started. Everybody killed on Bloody Sunday came from the Bogside. In the morning after Bloody Sunday, that Monday, Rossville Street was packed by quiet people. When people did talk, they talked in whispers. The state had maimed the Bogside community. Within a couple of months of Bloody Sunday, the never-ending source of our political ills, Stormont, was abolished. (McCann's language matches the revolutionary, Wolfe Tone, who described Ireland's connection with England as the 'never-failing source of all our political evils'.) That changed the constitutional position of course. There's no other atrocity in the forty years of the Troubles which marked so significant a plot point in the narrative of Northern Irish history. Of all the atrocities that pock mark the history of the last forty years, Bloody Sunday had that distinction, that grisly appalling distinction. People still demand the truth about Bloody Sunday.

Bloody Sunday was also the time at which it became impossible to argue for a socialist approach. If I suggested to anybody that they ought to seek a remedy for their grievances through the official constitutional channels, I would have been laughed at. The Parachute Regiment shot socialism off the streets.

MF: Why is it that so many significant figures came out of St. Columb's during these years?

EM: There had to be something about the experience which helps to explain it. Just a couple of years earlier than me, we had Heaney, we had Hume, we had Seamus Deane, Phil Coulter. We had Martin O'Neill. I think that one of the things that was distinctive about St. Columb's in those days is that St. Columb's was a pretty staid sort of order, a very conservative place, run by a very conservative church that saw the role of St. Columb's as sustaining that conservatism. Yet there came a sort of influx into St. Columb's of people who were full of excitement about the possibilities that were opening up before them and who had wonderment in their imaginations at being in a new place. St. Columb's didn't know how to handle this influx of people. The collision or abrasion between the way St. Columb's had seen itself on the one hand and, on the other, the expectations and attitudes of people who came from places like the Bogside and rural areas as well created sparks and some of the sparks caught fire, like Seamus Heaney and Seamus Deane. For St. Columb's to claim that this Catholic school produced Nobel prize-winners and great poets would be a wee bit like the medieval papacy claiming to have produced the great works of the Renaissance. To some extent it was a reaction against St. Columb's.

MF: What are your positive memories of the teaching you received at St. Columb's?

EM: Sean B. O'Kelly, who taught us English, was the man who sparked my love of literature. He would convey his own excitement and his own enthusiasm for literature. I remember 'getting' T.S. Eliot one day in O'Kelly's class, really getting it in a way that made me want to read more.

I encountered Gerard Manley Hopkins: 'The Kingfisher' and 'Glory be to God for Dappled Things'. All that wonderful, wonderful sprung rhythm sort of language. That came from St. Columb's. St. Columb's did give me some of the qualities, I suppose, which have helped me along the way and made my life fuller. So I do not like to be entirely negative about St. Columb's. Well I do. But it would be wrong.

Phil Coulter

Coulter excelled academically and musically in St. Columb's. The new legislation had opened grammar school to Coulter and his siblings, and he was marked out from his school days as a bright light. Pupils before 1947 paid ten pounds a year, but soon got scholarships. Talent scouts assessed boys for scholarships as horse-traders judge form.

Soccer is a recurring theme in Coulter's interview. It is easy to see why soccer has been important to Coulter all his life. Growing up, boys played football on the streets on a 'twelve half, twenty four the winner' basis. It was tribal stuff. Players represented their areas. They put down jumpers and coats to mark goals. After twelve goals to one side, they would change around – sometimes gaining or losing the aspect of the hill in the process. If the footballers stopped for tea, they stood to lose the street to another set of football teams. As one of Coulter's classmates remembers, they had 'an incredibly good youth'. Everyone

was deprived which meant that everyone shared. It was an open door community. Children were always recognised by their parentage: 'Oh, you are Paddy's son ... Arguably, things would be better if they turned back to community. The things modern society puts its faith in today – such as oil – are finite.' In Coulter's famous lyric about Derry he is scarcely being nostalgic. Speaking about an area recorded in Coulter's famous Derry song, one football star remembers, 'I ran home every day to the Creggan for lunch and ran back in time for the start of class. The bolt-hole for day-boys was the playing field.'

Coulter speaks in interview of how hard St. Columb's was for boarders and how removed day-boys were from their experience. Boarders constantly cadged food from day-boys. Boarders were scarcely held in higher esteem by St. Columb's. They were always hungry. Remembering 'the happiest days of our lives', one boarder said to me:

> 'The regime in St. Columb's was tougher than prison. At least prisoners have rights. There was no investigation. Human rights did not come into it. There were no rights in St. Columb's. What was worse was that authority was delegated to prefects.'

This particular student's first memories of St. Columb's were hunger and violence. Hunger hit first. A boy, who later became his best friend at the school, sat down with him on the first evening. They had been given a slice and a half of white pan, a smidgen of butter and a small spoonful of jam. They ate and then they wondered, in their naivety, what would be for tea. They had just eaten it. Boys soon learned to save some bread for morning and stick butter to the bottom of the desk. Occasionally someone would swipe his finger along the desk and steal the butter ration of ten boys.

As things began to open up, into the 1950s, certain teachers came into their own. One, Jack 'Rusty' Gallagher, produced good Shakespeare plays with Sean McMahon. Both Rusty and Sean McMahon exercised discipline, but students were not beaten for forgetting a line in the play. They knew there was a different way of disciplining people. Overall, some students have a positive recollection of the teachers as a body. Many of the teachers were a decent cross-section of humanity.

Coulter was a prominent thespian, acting alongside Heaney in *The Tempest*. Acting in Gilbert and Sullivan's *Pirates of Penzance*, Coulter said the lines, 'the policeman's lot is not a happy one'. Occasionally, St. Columb's boys would attend a Latin play staged by Campbell College, a Protestant school in Belfast. The play would come to Derry and they were allowed to attend. Boys would go to Magee College and speak with the Protestant boys. It was around this time that a woman, Mrs. Downey, was brought in to teach elocution at St. Columb's. Students humiliated her. They thought that women were weak. She actually laughed at some of the outrageous things that some of the boys said. One priest made overtures towards her. St. Columbs' monochrome masculinity was undergoing a change.

McCann remembers that Coulter was one of the actors in St. Columb's playing in Lady Gregory's *The Rising of the Moon*. A police officer uniform was required for one of the parts. As Coulter's dad was in the RUC, he was asked to provide one. Coulter came in the next day looking glum. He informed the teacher that he would be unable to supply a uniform for the play. 'Better a uniform with a hole in it,' one of the boys said and everyone laughed. But it was surely an uncomfortable moment for Coulter; and a foreshadowing of 1970's Northern Irish political modalities. By the 1970s, a boy whose father was an RUC man stood to be jeered in St. Columb's and would have had 'God Save the Queen' ironically sung to him by his classmates.

Families expected 'College Boys' to go to university and do well there. Coulter's eldest brother, Joe, became a doctor of divinity at a very young age. Coulter speaks of being let loose in Belfast in this interview. Even in his recreational activities, however, he was achieving something. Archer Bilk came to the Glee Club thanks to Coulter's excellent organisational skills. Coulter is remembered by younger boys for getting them a free day at St. Columb's, after winning the State Exhibition.

Coulter's commentary on Bloody Sunday is interesting because this interview traces Derry from being a placid place through to its explosion. Coulter's love song for his town takes us from the 1950s into the 1960s. His sympathy towards those who joined the IRA in its aftermath, given that his father was an RUC man, is remarkable.

Phil Coulter's song – his 'pay back to Derry' – starts with a stirring and defining image and ends with an evocation born out of the indomitable spirit of the people:

Now the music's gone, but they carry on,
For their spirits be bruised, never broken.
They will not forget but their hearts are set
For tomorrow they'll have peace once again.
For what's done is done and what's won is won
And what's lost is lost and gone for ever.
I can only pray for a bright, brand new day
In the town I loved so well.

MF: What is your background, Phil?

PC: I grew up in Abercorn Terrace. There were five kids. I suppose we were comfortable: we didn't have any great luxuries. We didn't have a car, but then nobody else had a car. We didn't have a TV. We had our three square meals and we had clothes on our back. We had two weeks holiday every year in a little cottage down in Lisfannon on the shores of the Swilly.

It was a house that was full of music. When there was ever an excuse in the neighbourhood for what we call in Derry 'A Big Night', they would have happened. We had the piano in the front room. Some of my earliest recollections would have been that – the music happening in the house. My father played the fiddle. He was from County Down. My mother, who was from the markets in Belfast, played the piano.

MF: Your father was in the RUC. Can you talk a little about that?

PC: My dad was a cop on the beat in my younger days and then became a plain-clothes cop in my teenage years. My father was as much a kind of community figure as anything else. He had a huge big bicycle that he used to cycle to work. He was six foot two. There were many people coming to the door with forms to seek Sergeant Coulter. There was a parade of characters to our front door, looking for my father to guide them through some bit of legislation to do with the dole or health benefits. It meant that I was on first name terms with practically every wino in Derry for a start. But in terms of my father and any kind of conflict as a Catholic in the RUC, I can honestly say that that never impinged on the family at all. We never felt that because he was a Catholic being in the RUC was an odd thing to do. He would have been a bit of a figurehead.

MF: Was there any stigma attached to being a Catholic in the force?

PC: This is an important thing to say: back at that time, in my primary years (in the Christian Brothers which would have been in the 1950s) there was not that edge. There was not that kind of confrontational thing between the Catholic community and the police that happened later on, by which stage my father was out of the police fortunately.

There certainly was a ceiling for Catholics in the RUC. There was a pattern that established itself over a number of years where a rookie detective would come to Derry and there would be a party. Maybe a year, eighteen months later, he'd be posted somewhere else and promoted. Then the next thing maybe the same guy would come back a few years later as a superintendent or something. As a Catholic, my dad had done very well to get to the rank of Detective Sergeant (looking back on it, it became obvious to me that he had got about as far as he was ever going to get). I didn't grow up in a household where we felt we were being victimised or my father was being marginalised because he was a Catholic. I think, at the end of the day, he probably was grateful for the fact that he had a good, steady pensionable job and was putting his three sons through St. Columb's.

MF: How was it for you to go to St. Columb's?

PC: My two brothers, Joe and Brian, had both trodden the same path. The Eleven Plus was your ticket into St. Columb's. You got the Eleven Plus: that was expected. It was kind of daunting to go up to St. Columb's – these big mountainy men from Bellaghy were a different breed from us city boys. We were weedy kind of chaps. We played soccer on the street, kicking a kind of battered old ball.

MF: What was expected from you at St. Columb's?

PC: St. Columb's had this great work ethic. You had to achieve academically and see how many State Exhibitions you could pull off against Portora or Methody. My middle brother Brian was a bit of a tearaway and scrambled through St. Columb's. He played it for laughs basically and his friends would have been all 'hard chaws'. Joe's pals would have been the studious types. So I was continually asked in my first term 'which of the two brothers are you like?' I was kind of in the middle. St. Columb's really instilled into you this sense (and I think it's stayed with me ever since) that if you have a talent, you have an obligation to do something with that talent.

The purpose of the college was to give an education which it did very effectively, and give us all that work ethic. It would have been a continuing mantra: don't squander your brain power.

If you used your brains and focused yourself on getting your results, what was available to you was third level education, which would not have been available to the previous generation. My father would never have been able to afford to pay to send me to university. So we were in that first or second intake of scholarship boys into St. Columb's and Queen's. That made you very aware that that was where the bar was set: that your expectation was to get a university scholarship. That emphasis on achieving was definitely a recurring theme at St. Columb's. Americans ask me – they would say that St. Columb's had two Nobel prize winners and all kinds of achievers in different areas – questions like, 'was it the school for the privileged?' My answer was it was the only school. St. Columb's was the only place in those days. That was it. There was a kind of religious expectation as well. St. Columb's was a junior seminary. It was set up really to send priests either to the Derry Diocese or to the missions. Certainly I gave serious thought to whether I had a vocation or not. Fortunately, it became obvious to me that that was not my route. I didn't at any time feel that I was under any duress. A vocation's not something you can shoehorn somebody into.

MF: What sort of musical education did you receive at St. Columb's?

PC: I would have been backwards and forwards at night – maybe three or four nights a week – I'd be back up for music classes or for choir practices. I had two music teachers. The man who taught me piano was a man called John Maultsaid, who undoubtedly was one of the best teachers (if not the best teacher) I ever had. My other music teacher was a man called Redmond Friel. He was a supreme musician and music just flowed out of this man. When he talked about music you could see the love of the music.

My fascination with pop music certainly would not have been encouraged in St. Columb's but I came out of St. Columb's with a great passion for music.

MF: What are your memories of sports in St. Columb's?

PC: Day-boys were soccer. We'd be closeted with these huge big farmers' sons from Desertmartin on the GAA pitch. I remember in my first year (you had to play Gaelic football in your first year) the priest who was in charge of Gaelic football in my year must have either had a cruel streak or a great sense of humour because he put me in goal. I was weedy with tiny wee legs, and my shorts were blowing in the wind. It was a freezing cold Saturday afternoon, and I'm stuck in the goal. It was a gravel pitch. There wasn't even any grass. I can remember this vividly. There was a kind of a huddle going on at the other end of the park and then I could see some of my teammates all being kind of flung out of this huddle which just revealed this mountainy guy. I remember his name too, he was from Dungiven, a big huge guy. He comes rumbling down towards me. I swear to God, I could feel the ground rumble underneath him. He's getting closer and closer and he's knocking players out of the way. My immediate defenders all of a sudden remembered to tie their bootlaces and there was nothing between me and him. He was coming closer and closer and I thought, oh my God. He dropped the ball and just let fly and hit it the most enormous punt. By some miracle I got in front of it, but he'd hit it so hard and I was so flimsy and light it lifted me off the ground and pinned me to the wall at the back in the mud and the wet. I kicked the ball out and I got through the rest of that game. I said this is not for me. I think I went to the teacher and I said, 'you know on Saturday afternoons I'm supposed to be practicing the piano, Father. Could you excuse me because the piano is what I do?' So the piano to me at that stage was a far better option than Gaelic football with these big guys from south Derry.

MF: What other contact did you have with the boarding community?

PC: Boarders would have had this perception of Derry boys as being dead wide. We thought we were cooler than them. These guys were bigger than you and they could have beat the lining out of you. You had to be twice as cute.

The boarders would have had a very strict regime. I certainly didn't envy them. I would be up of an evening time for piano lessons or music lessons, and I'd see them trooping into the refectory, then going back into the study. It never tempted me. I could go home at night and my mammy would cook the dinner. I remember when I'd go up in the evenings, I would have a bag of chips from the chippery on Bishop Street for some of my boarder pals. It was a bit like Stalag 17.

MF: What are your memories of the other participants in this film?

PC: I remember Heaney very well. We were in a couple of the school productions together. There used to be a Shakespearian play every year. I remember we did *The Tempest* and I played Ariel and Heaney played one of the parts. He was always very droll, very funny, and great company. The great tribute to Heaney is that when I meet Heaney these days he's the same Seamus Heaney: that kind of a laconic delivery that he has is as I remember him from St. Columb's.

McCann was the classic day-boy in St. Columb's because McCann was a fast talking smart-alec, far too lippy for his own good. But McCann is McCann and has remained that way. He's a one off, Eamonn. I do remember very, very well McCann's maiden speech at the debating society in the university. He came up a year after me. I just remember the confidence and the swagger. I thought there's an excellent Columb's boy. I found it very intimidating in my first year and I wouldn't have had the bottle to stand up and speak. We kind of clung together a little bit for safety because we knew we were well out of our depth. That didn't apply to McCann. McCann just strolled in there and just took the place on. A few years later he was actually the president of the debating society. I remember that feeling very well: that McCann definitely can cut the mustard here, no bother at all. He just had that great flair, that great eloquence, that great flow of words, quoting statistics. I remember feeling a little tinge of pride – he's one of our boys. He was head and shoulders above any other speaker at that Freshers' debate as they called it. He said, 'yeah, I'll have a piece of this'. He was great.

MF: How was it to be up in Belfast, in Queen's?

PC: A great adventure. It was like being let loose in the toy shop without the controls that you had at St. Columb's. Within my first term at Queen's I started my own band, and we'd never have got away with that in St. Columb's.

MF: Did you feel yourself to be part of the first generation to have gone through the Eleven Plus?

PC: That scholarship was open both to Catholics and Protestants. There were Protestants who were arriving in Queen's from similar backgrounds who would never have aspired to university but for the 1947 Education Act. There was a great sort of 'can do' attitude. I never felt at any stage marginalised by being a Catholic. We had this sense that we were the generation that was going to kind of dismantle all of that. In your social life, it was more important as to what your interests were, what your passions were. We would be the generation that maybe would change things down the road. And I think we probably did.

MF: How did 1947 modify or alter nationalists' agenda?

PC: To a large extent, nationalist politics up until then had been the politics of abstaining, the nationalists or the anti-partitionists walking out regularly from the council in Derry. This is a party which is built on being against something. With that generation there was a kind of realisation that the political set-up here is not right. It's unjust and it should be addressed. The way to do it is not to walk out of meetings, not to list the grievances but actually address the grievance, try to do something about it. So the whole civil rights thing would have been gaining momentum. In Queen's, for example, one of my flat-mates was Austin Currie. There would certainly be an argument for saying that that education act in the late '40s was a critical date in the evolution of Northern Ireland because it did produce people who, with the benefit of education, could argue their case and could stand up and say, 'if it's okay to have one man one vote in England why is it not right here?' We addressed the issues in a kind of logical way and argued a case rather than, as I say, protesting or abstaining. When the history of that period is written, you look back at the John Humes or the Austin Curries. That 1947 Education Act, affording third level education to that whole generation, was critical.

MF: And you Derry boys would have been particularly aware of the political set-up?

PC: I think those of us coming from Derry most assuredly would have been aware of gerrymandering and the lack of housing. You can't be from Derry, you can't be of that generation, and not be politically aware. It was part of the air that you breathed.

MF: Being a twenty year old in a third level institution and being aware of this situation, did you start to think about your father's occupation as a sort of enforcer of it? That the RUC was keeping this gerrymander in place?

PC: Fortunately, at that stage, he was no longer a part of it. I was certainly relieved that he wasn't part of it. That whole civil rights thing developed in 1968 and post-Duke Street [5 October 1968]; it would have been seriously uncomfortable to have had a father in the police force. I'm sure that would have been a very untenable position for him: that whole confrontational thing. I never felt that he was part of a structure that was like 'Croppies lie down'.

MF: You helped to found the Glee Club. How did that come about?

PC: That kind of grew out of guys from, like, St. Columb's, a few guys from Omagh, a few Belfast guys. We formed the Glee Club. American universities have glee clubs. They sing barber shop quartets. Amongst our aims was to promote the lesser arts amongst the intelligentsia. That's how serious we were.

I took over then as club president. We became the biggest society in the university, much to the consternation of the powers that be. What are these guys doing? Here were these jumped up boys, and a lot of them would have been those kind of maverick guys from the likes of

*The author in front of the helicopter used for aerial footage,
generously sponsored by Sean Quinn*

*The director of the film, Tom Collins, speaks to 'the boys' before filming –
(left to right) Coulter, Brady, McCann, Sharkey, Hume*

Preparing to film inside the church at St. Columb's

Filming the intereview with Shane Paul O'Doherty

Eamonn McCann in front of the college theatre
where he was accounted a good actor

Filming the college corridors

*The author, Deane, Heaney and Tom Collins
sharing a joke in front of the college*

*Deane and Heaney walking through the Bogside in front
of the iconic mural of Bishop Daly on Bloody Sunday*

Seamus Heaney getting ready to be interviewed

Seamus Deane sharing his views with the author

McCann, Sharkey and Coulter discuss the
North of their childhood over tea

Coulter teaching present-day St. Columb's boys about song-writing

Paul Brady tuning up at his studio

*'Ar nduthcas' or 'Our heritage', written on stained glass in the
former museum (later library) of St. Columb's*

*Hume and the author photographed in front of
Magee College where Hume is Professor Emeritus*

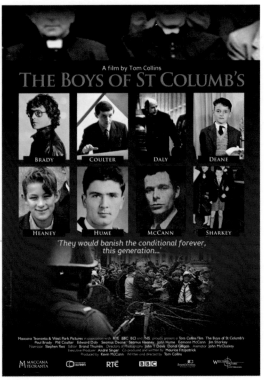

*The promotional poster for the film designed by the
producer, Kevin McCann*

St. Columb's. The music society and the jazz club had been fine for generations.

MF: It gave you confidence in terms of organising?

PC: The very fact that we were allowed in there, the very fact that we were doing what we wanted to do, did build a great 'can do' attitude: if you want to get a career in the music business how do you go about it? That is the $64,000 question. In my last year in Queen's as a rag week stunt somebody came to me, some bright spark in the rag week committee said, 'it'd be a great idea if we could make a student record'. Bear in mind this is 1964, before independent labels were even thought of. We recorded this track called 'Foolin' Time'. We got a lot of mileage out of it. Subsequently it was picked up by one of the big show bands. They were then going to London to record another bunch of songs and they asked me could I write them some more songs. I went across to London, and I met their agent. He saw me working with the band and he offered me a job. It was a momentous decision really: whether I should jump ship and take this job or shall I bite the bullet and go back, finish off in Queen's. I thought, what do you want more? Much to the displeasure of my parents, my family, and I'm sure all the staff at St. Columb's, I jumped ship and went to London. My ex-teachers were all shaking their heads. We'll never hear of him again, God knows what he's doing, playing in some strip club in Soho. I'd got to prove that this was the right move (not that I needed much encouragement to give it my best shot in London). It was therefore all the sweeter when my first real success was as high profile as it was in winning the Eurovision Song Contest. I sometimes afterwards kind of wished that I was in Derry watching it on TV rather than in Vienna. People who were in Derry were telling me that they were brought right into the streets celebrating: our boy's won the Eurovision. I remember two or three weeks after that the Mayor of Derry decided to give me a civic reception which consisted of a visit to the Mayor's parlour and a glass of dry sherry. The Mayor's car was sent up to Abercorn Terrace, to our little terraced house. We didn't have cars in the street at all in those days. So it was a major event, my dad and my mother in her best bib and tucker out into the back of the Mayor's car to drive down. For me to be celebrated in Derry by the Mayor and all that kind of respectability was incredibly important for my mother.

MF: You felt a little bit vindicated?

PC: Vindication I suppose would be the word. Last month when I was in New York, I was being interviewed. The interviewer was impressed that I'd had hits in the '60s and the '70s and the '80s and the '90s. He said, 'how do you account for that, the staying power?' And I said, 'that's easy, I turn up for work on Monday morning. It's what I do, it's my job', and I put that down to a large extent to that work ethic that I inherited in St. Columb's.

I was a Visiting Professor at Boston College for a number of years, in the music department there. You would have a class full of very

bright, very privileged, very talented kids. My opening pitch to them always was, 'do you know what your talent entitles you to? Nothing. Don't congratulate yourself because you're talented. Why? Because it had nothing to do with you. You inherited that from the genes of your parents. This is a gift from God. Congratulate yourself when you do something with the talent.'

MF: Can you speak a little about Derryness? You feel yourself to be a Derryman?

PC: Derryness is a very potent thing. I have a great sense of my Derryness. The hard-headedness to stick with something when it's not happening. That's what Derry people do. When people ask me, 'if you were to nominate one of your songs that you would like to be remembered for – would it be 'My Boy' for Elvis Presley or the Bay City Roller songs?' It would be, 'The Town I Loved So Well'. I would perceive that as being some kind of payback, to Derry. Derry is breathing through that song.

It's been recorded in thirty-seven different languages. One of the most bizarre manifestations of that was last year on the BBC television news, they showed a clip of a Japanese folk diva who travelled to Derry with fifty of her acolytes. They came to the Walls of Derry and she stood up on the Walls and the fifty were there and all of them sang 'The Town I Loved So Well' in Japanese. Now, that was the most surreal experience I ever had, just watching that on TV. I'm talking about the Creggan, the Moor and the Bog.

MF: The song, towards the end, in its fourth verse, shows the history of Derry from the civil rights into Bloody Sunday and its aftermath. Can you describe how you came to write this song and the sort of feelings you had?

PC: I was producing The Dubliners at the time. That meant that I had in the loop Luke Kelly, who could breathe life into any song that I would write. Kelly could bring, apart from a great voice, an integrity to the song. He wouldn't cheapen it.

I happened to be in Derry on the day that internment was introduced [on 9 August 1971, under the auspices of Prime Minister Brian Faulkner, internment without trial was introduced in Northern Ireland. The European Court of Human Rights later ruled that the British army subjected internees to 'degrading and inhuman treatment' – M.F.]. I saw the kind of absence of any specific intelligence. If you played Gaelic football, if you spoke Irish, if you went to *Cheildh* dances or if you had any kind of an Irish Nationalist identity, you were fair game – a terrorist as far as they were concerned. So there were guys being hauled out of bed at four o'clock in the morning for no good reason. I was incensed, as was everybody else (this was before Bloody Sunday). This was the rape of the city. People were frogmarched away to interment camps. Their wives and kids were going, 'what's going on here?' My knee-jerk reaction was to write a song called 'Free the People', which was an anti-internment song. A few weeks after, we did a big anti-internment rally in Dublin. The song was the kind of centre point of it. I got Richard Harris to come across. Hume came down. Austin Currie came down. We were into the early '70s, post-Duke Street [5 October 1968], just seeing the traumatic change. Derry had always been an upbeat kind of place. There was music going on and people had a bit of a spring in their step. There were a lot of men on the dole, okay. But they went out and walked the dog. This pall of gloom descended on the place over those early 1970s. On one of my visits back, I was on the fringe of a riot in Waterloo Place and saw the water canon being used and I thought, 'this is just completely indiscriminate'. It was a build up of a lot of frustration.

I think I wrote the tune in maybe a couple of weeks. But the lyric took me most of a year to put together. I didn't want to write another rebel song. We'd got plenty of them, and that would have added nothing at all to the debate. I wanted to write a song which was essentially a love song about my place and a song that decried violence from whatever source. I didn't want to fudge it at all. I can vividly remember when I unveiled the song for the very first time to Luke Kelly. It was in the most unlikely surroundings, in a two star hotel in Sheffield. The Dubliners were playing in a working man's club there, and we were due to go into the studio within the next couple of weeks. It was on a wet Monday afternoon, I think, in a twin-bedded room in this not very salubrious hotel, Kelly sitting on one bed and I'm sitting here with the guitar and my eyes closed. I sang 'The Town I Love So Well' from beginning to end. Somebody like Luke Kelly had an encyclopedic knowledge of folk music. Kelly would also have been a strong socialist. I finished the

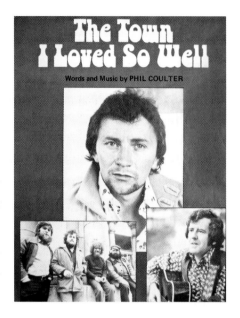

song, not really knowing the reaction I was going to get, but knowing this is as good as I can make it. I finished the song with the last chord and I opened my eyes and I looked at Luke Kelly, and there were tears in Luke Kelly's eyes. From that moment, I knew this song has got something special.

MF: Can you remember where you were when Bloody Sunday happened?

PC: I was in America when I heard about Bloody Sunday. And if the sense of having been violated and your town being violated and your people being violated, with the introduction of internment – that was small beer compared to the feeling that you had at Bloody Sunday. It was one of disbelief. You'd think, 'God almighty, this can't be happening': shock, horror, anger. For moderate people in Derry, moderate Catholics, that day would have definitely provoked them into the corner. I know of some people that it did, that it turned them from being kind of middle-of-the-road sort of nationalists to being terrorists by the definition of some people. The effect that it had on Derry people – that to me was, was the biggest trauma. The massacre that it was, apart from being such a horrendous injustice, intensified any kind of middle-of-the-road thinking. It propelled a huge number of the population into taking a harder stance. Do you know what? If I'd been living in Derry I might have been one of them.

My one great regret was that I did not fly back from America for the funerals. I should have been at the funerals, just to pay my respects. I was in the middle of a recording project with a studio full of musicians in Los Angeles. Bloody Sunday is something that people in Derry really can't stomach. There hasn't been any closure on that. In the heart's core of Derry people, they still think that's unfinished business.

MF: You got heavily involved with Derry FC when it was in dire straits. Can you talk a little about that?

PC: Derry were excluded from football in the North of Ireland, wrongly so in the eyes of a lot of people, including myself. After a period of being out of senior soccer, Derry people, being pragmatic, said well, 'if they don't want us to play soccer in the North let's play soccer in the South'. People said, 'what, are you crazy, we're not even in the south geographically or politically'. 'It doesn't matter, we'll make it happen', and we did.

Within a couple of years we were winning everything and there were buses leaving Derry in their twenties. There were even non-alcoholic buses, Pepsi buses. They would drive to Cork, and then on the way into Cork they would find a pub on the outskirts and they would go in there and maybe have a bowl of soup. It was a huge community thing. In the dark days, it was a great place for Derry people still to celebrate their Derryness. I was asked if I would become club president. It was a figurehead job. It was a kind of rocky time financially, but we managed to pull ourselves through it. Voices said maybe we should just wind it up. Maybe we should reconstitute it as something else. But by a combination of strokes – we got, for example, Martin O'Neill (who was then managing Celtic) to send over a Celtic team which was a huge night for the Brandywell. I remember him saying, 'this is a really curious experience because for years when I was a boarder at St. Columb's I used to stand up there at that wall and look over at the Brandywell on the nights of the floodlit games'.

I got Alex Ferguson, who I'm friendly with, to send over a Manchester United team. He said, 'Phil, I'm not going to send you the top guys, but I'll send you a Man United team. There'll be few faces in there they'll recognise but it'll be a Man United team'. I said, 'Alex, that'll do nicely'. And John Hume I think got Barcelona or Real Madrid to come. So we had a couple of big paydays. I ran a few golf pro-am things. We just got our shoulders to the wheel and began to get things up and running again.

I have a nineteen year old son who is currently the reserve keeper for Dundalk United. I didn't manage to become Charlie Heffron [Derry City FC goalkeeper of yore] but my son is now going down that road.

He's working towards a soccer scholarship in the United States. If he got a chance to play for Derry City he'd be there in a heartbeat because that's in his blood. As a kid, I used to take him up to the games.

MF: It's interesting you mentioned Martin O'Neill because in the course of my research – I am not from the North of Ireland – I learned that Martin O'Neill was offered the OBE as were you. He accepted it, and you refused it. You felt that it wasn't you?

PC: Well everybody's got to make his own call. Martin accepted it and Pat Jennings accepted it and a lot of very good people, people I respect, accepted it. I just didn't feel comfortable with it. I can't give any logical reason for that. It didn't sit comfortably with me. The fact that it was during the tenure of Maggie Thatcher may have very well had something to do with it. It might have been construed that I'm a Maggie Thatcher supporter. My ego was in good enough shape. I didn't think I needed an OBE. I didn't want to impress the postman. What I do is make records and write songs. It's great to get a Grammy nomination because that's from people within the industry. Everybody's got to make their own call on that. I don't think any of the lesser of Martin, for example, or Pat Jennings for accepting an OBE.

MF: St. Columb's of today has now relocated. Can you explain how and why that happened?

PC: I had mixed feelings when the Bishop Street campus of St. Columb's semi-relocated down to the Buncrana Road. It was just that the numbers were too big. Those six years up at St. Columb's were a very formative time in my life. I do have an affection for the place. I thought it's not going to be St. Columb's anymore. It became Lumen Christi. I totally understand there's now a new St. Columb's because the demand is bigger and the facilities in the Buncrana Road are sensational. There's now a whole new college, Lumen Christi, which is carrying on a great tradition.

I'm certainly looking forward to walking up those Walks again in Bishop's Street; but equally so I'm looking forward to getting a feel of the new St. Columb's. As the song says, nothing is forever and no-one stays the same.

MF: Did you succeed in spite of St. Columb's College or because of St. Columb's College?

PC: Did I succeed in spite of St. Columb's College or because of St. Columb's College? I would have no doubt that whatever combination of talent, tenacity, temperament and work ethic I have, I would owe that to St. Columb's. Not that St. Columb's spotted in me a future song writer, record producer, orchestrator and put me on that path – they didn't, because they weren't in the business of doing that. But it certainly equipped me with enough academic confidence to go to Queen's and hold my head up and fight my corner. It certainly gave me enough determination that whatever it would take, that I would get through; and I couldn't have done it if I hadn't had those two great music teachers who had, on one hand, an ability to assimilate the music and an ability to address the whole structure and discipline of music (whether that be harmony, counterpoint, orchestration) combined with just a great love and a great passion for music. I certainly owe St. Columb's a great debt. I would hazard a guess and say that the one thing we all have in common is that work ethic. I would say that that's consciously or unconsciously something which we imbibed during five or six years in St. Columb's. Seamus Heaney didn't become the poet that he is by sitting on his backside. John Hume didn't become the statesman that he became by sitting on his backside.

I learned that you have to go out and make your own way. The notion that if you want to make something happen, don't wait for other people to do it. If you've got brains, use them.

MF: And you are among illustrious company.

PC: I'm very proud of Heaney. I'm very proud of Hume. I'm very proud of Deane. Very proud of McCann. I'm very proud of Martin O'Neill. Very proud of Eddie Daly, who by anybody's standards is a hero. What Eddie Daly did for many, many years was Trojan: running concerts at St. Columb's Hall to keep people up in the dark days; and his actual heroics on Bloody Sunday. Putting that caring face on the Catholic Church, a man with a common touch. I think he's a real hero, Eddie Daly.

MF: You would have been behind Deane and Heaney at Queen's. Do you remember them there?

PC: They were the kind of cool Derry guys. They were a few years ahead of me. That visiting professor thing in Boston College – I remember asking Seamus Heaney, what's the story on this stuff? Seamus Heaney said, 'Yeah, do it'.

MF: That work ethic you mentioned is absent in the music industry now?

PC: There's a culture at large now, where kids think they're entitled to be in show business, you know. They think all they have to do is turn up for one of these reality talent shows and they've this attitude, 'it's my turn'. I keep telling Louis Walsh that none of his bands have ever come close to the Bay City Rollers, because the Bay City Rollers were a global phenomenon. Thinking back to Jimmy Durante, he would have gone on and done his shtick. Then he would have worked his way up until he became the top of the bill.

MF: So what does it take to be a successful song-writer in your estimation?

PC: Somebody like Franz Schubert was, in his day, a songwriter. That's what he did for a living. He'd get up in the morning and there was nothing in the cupboard. There was no bread, there was no milk, there was no porridge. 'God, bit strapped for cash, I think I'd better write a few songs.' It's not something that is demeaning for a musician. It's not something that dilutes your musicianship at all.

When I first became a pop song writer, we had a contract where we had to write six songs every two weeks. Every second Friday we went into a little studio with six brand new songs. When you're writing that much material, you learn the craft of songwriting. It was pure pop, pop songs – three chords, four chords at the most. We sold millions of records. There's no such thing as a natural songwriter. You're born with a good ear. If you want to be a songwriter you have to have a flair for language and you have to have a fascination for rhyming and for rhythm. It's a craft that you have to learn. It's like the craft of writing poetry.

Ask Seamus Heaney, he'll tell you. It's a craft that you have to learn by studying other poets and working at it yourself. If you want to be a silversmith, you could have the most talented eye and have very creative hands, but you have to work with a master silversmith who'll tell you how this all works and how you can create these things. I was fluent in the grammar of music. And it's only that that gives you the confidence to be able to kind of take the music.

Having a career and passion is not mutually exclusive. I think you can't have a career unless you have a passion. You don't have to have yachts in the South of France. You don't have to have Rolls Royces and you don't have to have big houses with staff. If you get up on a Monday morning looking forward to what you're going to do that week, you are successful. To do what you really want to do for a living is the ultimate thing. Being a professional soccer player's not easy, being an actor's not easy, being a fashion designer's not easy. Anything easy is very seldom worth talking about.

Testimony of an IRA Volunteer – Shane Paul O'Doherty

This book is an examination of the North of Ireland from 1947–1972. The following testimony – that of an IRA volunteer who attended St. Columb's in the late 1960s, just as the North was beginning to disintegrate – is a glimpse of the next generation and the struggles of a quite different nature that it encountered. Coulter moots in his interview that when the latent violence in the North was unleashed a sympathy for it was almost the most human response; also that the police force, of which his father had been a member, had lost any claim to legitimacy it might have had. Coulter's compelling perspective is suggestive of impulses that dominated the next phase of Northern Irish politics. This inter-chapter is intended to give voice to the violence that later prevailed in the state.

I passed the dreaded Eleven Plus and entered St. Columb's to the extremities of the yaps' first day. You were bullied and dragged into the toilets and ducked down the toilets and flushed numerous times. There was never any question that I would pass the Eleven Plus. My dad was a teacher in the Christian Brothers' school next door.

To pass the Eleven Plus was the aim of your whole life. My best friend of my early childhood, Raymond Kinsella, from Queen Street, Dr Kinsella's son, failed and was unceremoniously packed off to a boarding school somewhere and I never saw him again. So the Eleven Plus divided me from my childhood best friend.

It was a certain pride to get in initially and wear the blazer. It was interesting to cross the Bogside four times a day in a school blazer because not everybody in the Bogside got into St. Columb's College. It was certainly a class issue: I had to cross the full length of the Lecky Road. There were groups of lads who weren't fond of the St. Columb's

College blazer. You'd get a bit of ribbing. I was fairly well known from the Christian Brothers.

I was well-received initially because my brothers had done well in swimming at St. Columb's. My father was teaching next door in the Christian Brothers' for close to forty years. My grandfather was probably a head of the Knights of Columbanus in the city. My mother's brother, Canon Danny Doherty, was a priest in the Glasgow Archdiocese. The reason he was in the Glasgow Archdiocese is that just before his final exams in St. Columb's College he'd had a row with the college authorities and was unable to go on for priesthood in the Derry diocese.

I was thirteen when 'The Battle of Bogside' happened. I had to cross that area four times a day, whether there was a riot on or whether there wasn't. I picked my way through the debris, rocks, the RUC and the rioters. In a college uniform, people would just assume you weren't a participant. I always found it odd: 'The Battle of Bogside' occurring in 1968 when I was thirteen; British troops arriving on the streets of Derry when I was fourteen; one of my best friends shot dead when I was sixteen, Eamonn Lafferty, and another of my friends shot dead a few days later in the Waterside, Jim O'Hagan, more of my friends shot dead in early 1972; the community brought to its knees by the Troubles; this was never mentioned in St. Columb's College. It was just this acre of other-ness, alienated from its own, from its own city. You could never go in and say, 'my best friend was shot dead a few weeks ago'. It was just this other place apart from the Bogside. Imagine when I was twelve there were civil rights marches throughout the city, factory girls protesting in the city centre, huge sit-down protests in the Guildhall. All these events were never alluded to in the college; the civil rights movement, never mentioned; the ravished streets and the community in the Bogside, never mentioned.

I and others began to flirt with joining the IRA when we were fifteen. A number of us approached what was then the Official IRA. Much later we joined the Provisional IRA through two well-known people in the Waterloo Street area. This happened when we were fifteen years of age. Going on sixteen, we had been incendiarising the city centre. Here we were joining the IRA at fifteen while going to school every day, and unable to communicate with anybody in St. Columb's College that the circumstances were dire on the streets. And this was before Bloody

Sunday; imagine the feeling when we were seventeen years of age, some of us having drifted away from the IRA for some time ... On Bloody Sunday I was so close to the paratroopers, but my St. Columb's College cross-country skills got me out of there through bullets hitting walls and past people who were being shot dead. In the aftermath of that we were all back knocking on the door of the IRA again saying, 'take us back, let us hit back at these bastards'.

When a terrible event happens in an American college or university now, they say that the school has to mark that this happened, has to somehow or other engage with the students. It was like 'The Battle of Bogside' never happened for St. Columb's College. I was carpeted by that president and I felt a real weight and disapproval and sneering of authority.

The authorities at St. Columb's looked down their noses at riff-raff from the ghettos who had been brought into St. Columb's. These ghetto boys landed in the college, bringing with them a whole raft of social problems. Events on the streets were contrary to the status quo and they endangered authority, and endangered the Catholic support for the status quo in Northern Ireland.

When one of our classmates was illegally beaten up by the British army and unfairly charged with a riotous assault, which he never in fact practiced, and was given six months in Crumlin Road jail; when Dermott McNabb was so treated, St. Columb's College, in its greatest act of generosity to the Bogside, took him back in without any question and he continued his studies.

I well remember working for my 'O' levels in 1971. I heard the perfect rattle off a Thomson machine gun. And I remember it vividly, sitting there thinking I know that's a Thomson machine gun that's just fired. I probably know who fired it. If anything happens to these friends of mine today, after they fire it or when they're firing it, here I am sitting holding a book. The whole education question for me became irrelevant.

It was my misfortune once to be attacked and beaten up by British soldiers in October 1972. I unfortunately wrote a letter to the *Derry Journal* where I decried the British soldiers who beat me up. There was shock in St. Columb's College. On the Friday that the letter appeared in the *Derry Journal* a prefect was sent to bring me before the president, who was utterly horrified that (a) a St. Columb's College boy would write a letter to a newspaper; (b) would complain about security forces beating him up; (c) that the schoolboy would've lost the plot to such an extreme degree as to mention in a newspaper events on the streets. After that letter appeared I was no longer wanted in St. Columb's College.

I well remember the shock and the horror in the college (almost like a disease had arrived) when news filtered in that Andy Hinds was holding a placard at the front gate in a protest for a student union or something. I remember the shock and the horror in the college at this, and his immediate expulsion from St. Columb's College.

St. Columb's was Castle Catholics at books, Castle Catholics at education. The only single protest that anybody in St. Columb's ever took part in was the 1966 protest for the setting up of the second university in Derry. I think the car cavalcade that made its way to Stormont contained a number from St. Columb's College.

My last memory of the college is that a number of British soldiers were working on the roof of the gas yard. A car was produced, and a driver and a support person. And I entered the college grounds carrying an Armalite rifle. We made our way to the back of St. Columb's, near the tower. And from there it seemed that the soldiers on the roof of the gas yard were really, really close as they were working on this observation tower or something. I fired a full magazine of Armalite bullets at these soldiers. I distinctly remember rushing back to the car, getting in the car, but contrary to all IRA rules of engagement or behaviour, we drove very slowly down the drive, out the gates, to Bishop Street with the Armalite rifle sticking out the window. And I just remember seeing priests in soutanes running to see what this shooting was in the grounds. And hundreds of schoolboys running.

I don't think St. Columb's College was the breakthrough for people who became prominent in Northern Ireland. I think the school that prepared many for the breakthrough in Northern Ireland was the Christian Brothers'. The Christian Brothers' educated and trained the great proletarian unwashed, got them through the Eleven Plus and presented them into St. Columb's College. Seamus Heaney was always going to be a poet. Seamus was a product of the Bellaghy hinterland, nothing to do with Derry City, completely unrelated to it. People like Seamus Heaney had the germ of genius and brilliance in them when they were back on the farm.

As my classmates proceeded to prepare for their 'A' Levels in June 1973, I was preparing to bomb London for the whole summer, quite alone, with letter bombs and time bombs. I was a solo IRA operator. The bombing part of the operation you'd do alone. I executed that in the summer of 1973 at the age of eighteen. That was *my* 'A' Level. And I felt my A grade in my 'A' Level was getting a letter bomb into 10 Downing Street – I was the only IRA volunteer ever to achieve that. I felt at the time that that was the 'A' Level I owed the Brits and I owed London. And blowing up Reginald Maudling, who had been in charge of Home Affairs during Bloody Sunday, with a letter bomb that same summer was my other A grade achievement at that time. At that age, the sorry fact is, that was my pride. I often remember sitting playing my BSR record player and listening to the Rolling Stones, 'You Can't Always Get What You Want', thinking I could die this evening, and it didn't worry me or faze me at all. It's a tragedy that young people my age went through that and volunteered themselves to the IRA again and again. It's obviously a tragedy when you look back at young lives blighted. The sorry fact is that if I were back in time and these events rolled out again, I'd do it all again. At that young age you don't have the luxury of hindsight and maturity and a mature religious sense or a mature appreciation of human rights.

It was a very conscious decision for me to park the studies. I knew that within a few short years I'd either be dead or in prison. I knew in prison I could get back to study. By my twenty-first birthday I had been given the boon of thirty life sentences and twenty years for the London letter bomb and time bomb campaign. It was in the British prisons – Wormwood Scrubs mainly, and later Long Kesh and Maghaberry Prison – that I got back into study. I decided I didn't want to be in an English university while bombs were still going off in England, so I applied to Trinity College Dublin.

Within a few days of my release from Maghaberry prison, after fourteen and a half years in Her Majesty's institutions, I entered Trinity.

The sneering of the upper echelons of the priestly caste at St. Columb's towards me and towards others in my year gave you kind of an inner strength. You gained a certain strength: how to stand on your own two feet and make incredibly dangerous life-changing decisions entirely on your own because there was no mentor. It prepared you for fourteen and a half years of equally sneering treatment from the British prison authorities. There was a linkage between Catholic Derry and British prisons: the *Derry Journal* newspaper was the only paper in Ireland that never mentioned that my book [*The Volunteer: A Former IRA Man's True Story*] was on the bestseller list. I wanted to also explain that a person could grow and change beyond IRA membership, IRA volunteer status, and become a citizen once again. Prison enabled me to write the book. It was cathartic for me to express to the world: here's my story.

I've always wrestled with Catholicism and the Catholic faith, and would've been marked in prison by my comrades as someone who went for the Gospel, went for the Catholic teaching and gave up arms struggle purely on Catholic grounds. I took three years out of my life recently to go back into a seminary and deal with issues of priesthood and so on.

I spent fourteen and a half months naked in solitary in Wormwood Scrubs when I refused to wear the criminal uniform. I think in total I spent three and a half years in solitary in prisons in England, protesting to get back to Northern Ireland. I had to confront the four Gospels. I had to confront prisoners' rights and this led me to human rights. I had to confront the horrible fact that for all the passion, frankly, the violence was wrong. I had to find the strength in prison to express publicly, to comrades, to the media, to the world at large that I felt sucked into the armed struggle. We jumped into politics. I had to learn the strength to say that in the English prisons, and I was not a little tutored by the solitary ways I learned in St. Columb's.

James Sharkey

Sharkey's great-grandmother, who hailed from north Donegal, spoke no English. English was so alien to her that on the first day when she brought her son to school, she immediately took him out again – hearing a strange, foreign language being spoken inside the doors. The next generation could speak more English, but Irish was still strong. One of this generation, Mary Ann Boyle, left Donegal for Derry to work in a shirt factory. This was Sharkey's mother. Although born in Derry, Sharkey has retained an affection for his mother's homeplace all his life.

Speaking of North Inishowen, Sharkey remembered:

'I spent all my summers in Urris from as early as I can remember staying mostly with my cousins, the McGonigals, in Dunaff and I started making the journey from Derry to Clonmany unaccompanied from the age of 10. In 1955, the first time I came here on my own, I had three instructions from my mother. The first was not to get lost – under no circumstances was I to get lost – as if I would plan to do so. The second was to tell anybody who asked me that I was one of Mary Ann Boyle's. She was sure that would make a difference if I did get lost. The third was to go to the house of Hughie Farren who was a taxi driver here in the fifties with a big trade in Urris and give him 6d. to take me out to Dunaff.'

Despite the differences engendered by the border, the Inishowen Peninsula was very close in many ways to Derry. Moville's natural centre is Derry City rather than Letterkenny. As travel was uncommon, customs officers stamped passes when people crossed the boarder. Antipartition agitation was strong in Inishowen but, as Sharkey says in the interview, the Troubles caused a degree of separation between the two areas that otherwise had a natural affinity.

Some boys from Southern primary schools went to St. Columb's but many of the rest emigrated or started to work early. Northerners didn't pay fees if they passed the Eleven Plus. Even in the case of those who did not pass the Eleven Plus in the North, a greater proportion of boys (than would have been the case in the South) went to technical school, the school lower in rank than grammar school.

In his interview, Sharkey speaks of the build up to the Eleven Plus examination. He sat in on Saturday mornings at the Christian Brothers' School doing intelligence tests in preparation for the Eleven Plus. (Italian children were forced to attend schools and boot camps on Saturdays for extra tuition during Mussolini's reign. They called it *Sabato fascista*.)

For all the brutality of the Christian Brothers School – by many accounts, it was the toughest school in the area – it was one of the best schools for gaining Eleven Plus examination successes. The focus on the Eleven Plus was absolute. Other schools were more arbitrary and not doing the Eleven Plus was more common, partly through a student's own negligence and partly the negligence of the teacher.

Sharkey speaks of the great pride that went with entry to St. Columb's. In a street of 120 houses, three or four boys would go to St. Columb's in a typical year. They were not the elite, but they had gone further than many of their peers. They had a nice blazer and that showed everyone that they were at the college. It gave the boy's family a reflected glory. The older community was especially in awe of their going to grammar school. In Derry people always visited each other's homes. Mothers would say, 'you know our Michael is at the college ... come in here and say hello Michael'. Nobody referred to the school as St. Columb's

– it was the college. Back then, expectation came almost exclusively from family rather than the media, as is the case in the contemporary world.

If stories of young boys getting hammered did not have a factual basis, some stories of St. Columb's would be genuinely funny. For example, one priest would make latecomers put their hands in cold water so that they would feel the sting of the strap all the more harshly. The same priest once sent a boy, whose grandfather was a cobbler, to his grandfather's shop to get a new strap. The boy dutifully ran the errand but, when he returned, the priest felt the need to try out the new strap. So he gave the boy six on each hand.

Sharkey makes the important distinction between the Junior Cycle and Senior Cycle at St. Columb's. Once the Senior Cert started, boys taking the exam could study in their rooms. This custom once led to a dozen boys or so starting a poker and smoking club in a classroom. Although they did not gamble, when they were discovered they were expelled – with only two weeks to go until the end of their time at St. Columb's. However, they were allowed to return to sit their exams – which was seen as a generous concession. Students over the age of fifteen could smoke in the 'reefing room'. In the reefing room at St. Columb's they smoked their own cigarettes. It was not customary to share. Once the boys happened to sing rebel songs in the room and they were punished for that.

Many from St. Columb's started to go to UCD because they were aged seventeen and eighteen years was the required entry age for Queen's. About half a dozen of St. Columb's boys went to UCD from St. Columb's in 1963. In Dublin they were inhibited and shy to begin with but they soon got used to life in the bigger city. On one particular Christmas Eve during university, returning from Dublin to Derry by train, Sharkey and a friend wondered what they had done. They had left bustling Dublin and were now staring down a completely vacant Foyle Street in Derry.

One time Jude Collins was driving Sharkey home from Dublin for a break. He picked up Sharkey on O'Connell Street with his girlfriend (later to be his wife). Collins stopped in his homeplace for tea and he left Sharkey alone with his (Collins') taciturn father. When he came back, Sharkey had started to talk to him about some far-flung area in Ulster and he got Collins' father to speak more than Collins had ever heard in his life. Sharkey still has that disarming openness and easy manner. At UCD he would not hold people's gaze. He stood at the radiator and kept his hands in his pockets. Now, the best of Sharkey comes out. He looks at his man. As Willie Melaugh, Professor at the University of San Francisco and a former classmate of Sharkey's, observed, 'at the end of a conversation with Jimmy, you'll have told him everything and he'll have told you nothing'.

One classmate of Sharkey's remembers, when he was very small, his father say that the 1947 Education Act was 'the seed of the downfall of Stormont' (the Stormont Government was prorogued in 1972). The great disciplined education taught them to solve problems and to write well. But their education had political significance and it took on more of that significance with every step. The almost mythic juxtaposition of the 1947 Education Act with the fall of the government (that was keeping Catholics under the thumb) was communicated to the children from the start.

When Sharkey was a teacher in 1968/9, the St. Columb's students organised a 'sit-in' and many in the staff room opposed it, but Sharkey found himself closer to the feeling of the boys. (Seamus Heaney in the same year marched shoulder-to-shoulder with Queen's students in Belfast during their campaign for civil rights.)

While it was revolutionary for a Catholic to hit the streets in the Northern Ireland of the 1960s, it was also a confirmation of feelings within the Catholic community. For Protestant members of the 'Eleven Plus Generation', to align themselves with civil rights demonstrators was – apart from a defiance of the law, as it also was for Catholics – to break with values that the Protestant tradition had long cherished. Basic democracy (voting, employment and housing parity) in the North of Ireland had such a difficult birth mainly because of the problem many Protestants had imagining their tradition incorporating an enlightened working class. This had wider implications for the union with Britain: the introduction of the British army (1969) and, later, the proroguing of Stormont (1972) in the wake of Bloody Sunday were direct results of the intransigence of unionists. It is in this context that Sharkey's comment, 'tragically a failure of unionism was the inability to absorb that generation', should be understood.

Catholics countered unionism, eventually, by hitting the streets and singing together. They were greatly inspired by the civil rights movement in America and they would sing:

We Shall Overcome

'We shall overcome, we shall overcome,
We shall overcome someday;
Oh, deep in my heart, I do believe,
We shall overcome someday.

The truth shall make us free, the truth shall make us free,
The truth shall make us free someday;
Oh, deep in my heart, I do believe,
The truth shall make us free someday.'

Apart from McCann, Sharkey was the only one of 'the boys' to have been on Craigavon bridge (the first civil rights demonstration on 5 October 1968) and on the Bloody Sunday march (30 January 1972). His analysis of those two events in Derry, as well as his interpretation of Northern Irish history generally, is what distinguishes this interview.

Catholics were nearly all united in their will to change things in 1968. By 1972, they had been pressured into taking political positions which diverted them from their common goal. Sharkey makes the valid point that Protestant support at an early stage for civil rights would have fortified the movement.

October 5th began Sharkey's involvement with the civil rights movement. He thinks that the importance of October 5th is still not fully perceived. In this light, his knowledge of Ulster, his judgment of reciprocity between countries and regional policies, can be understood.

Sharkey's huge endeavour to mark the four hundred year anniversary of 'The Flight of the Earls' included inviting former St. Columb's men Hume and Brady to the St. Patrick's Day celebrations in Switzerland. Unfortunately, due to an accident the night before, Hume could not travel. But the Ambassador read Hume's speech wonderfully and in the first person. Following the trail of the Earls through the Swiss Alps, there was a re-enactment of the march by a troupe of actors on the slopes of the Alps. Later, at a church, the Ambassador read the gospel in Irish. And at another ancient, small church he unveiled a plaque made from the green granite of the mountain.

The acting troupe, who were performing Brian Friel's play *Making History*, followed the trail of the last Princes of Ireland. When performing in Derry, the joke about O'Doherty, the sheep-stealer in *Making History*, had great resonance. Friel, a teacher in Derry for many years and now living in Donegal, was attentive to the nuances of surnames in his plays: Dohertys would be laughing up their sleeves at the O'Doherty clan being sent up. In Derry the phrase, 'Yeah, and your granny is O'Doherty', means 'yeah, right'. But the last word on the Dohertification of Derry belongs to McCann. He tells a story of a Chinaman who fetches up in Derry, earning his living by driving a cab. He is so fond of the place and the people that he takes the name O'Doherty. One day he is asked by a customer, Ming, to drive him across the border. At the checkpoint, a British soldier demands their names. 'O'Doherty' said the Chinaman; 'Ming', said the Derryman. They were let go after an hour.

In *Making History*, Friel writes that the English wanted to build forts from Dundalk to Sligo. That play is set at the turn of the seventeenth century and it was what gave Ulster its new identity – in the psychic and political sense rather than the geographical. The arbitrary partitioning of the land did not put paid to a pan-Ulster heritage. Sharkey sees in the *Field Day Anthology* a deep sensitivity and knowledge of the Irish diaspora, a knowledge that existed everywhere north of the line from Sligo to Dundalk. Students had a higher consciousness of this heritage for having gone to St. Columb's.

Sharkey exhibits a collectedness and a clarity that prickly Northern politics requires. The hawk's eye view – the only way to at once act and to transcend the complex difficulties of the present tense – is seen in his mediation on the bridge on October 5th. The situation was too volatile to be handled with force: it required diplomacy and sensitivity. October 5th had the unfortunate effect of entrenching unionist psychology: they could not give in to it and, fatally, Britain bolstered them in their opposition.

Sharkey speaks about decolonisation, the global phenomenon of Britain (and other countries) losing its colonies. Joyce had written many decades before about the repressed psyche, the uncreated conscience, the generations to shuffle off the effect of colonisation. After the war, Britain's grip on the colonies started to loosen. Attlee's Labour government embraced a decolonising agenda. The Commonwealth trade relationship between colonial units was offered as a substitute. It delegates authority to individual colonial units. The failure of the established middle class of Derry to absorb this new generation of Catholics forms a counterpoint to Sharkey's comment about unionism. When the North exploded this inability to engage with young boys who were tempted to arms was thrown into sharper focus.

As Ambassador of Ireland, Sharkey placed major emphasis on the understanding of another nation's culture as a means to understanding the country. 'Japanese professors used to live in the place,' as someone noted of the Tokyo residence. Sharkey was acting Irish Ambassador to Scandinavia when Hume won the Nobel Prize in Oslo in 1998. (Deane was present when Heaney received his Nobel Prize in Stockholm in 1995.)

But Sharkey's achievement goes beyond diplomacy. He has inspired Seamus Heaney, who wrote the following poem on the occasion of Sharkey becoming one of St. Columb's alumni. 'This was a little informal greeting I sent to Jim Sharkey when he became an Alumnus Illustrissimus of St. Columb's College' – Seamus Heaney. [He reads]:

14 October 2005
Alumnus Illustrissimus

From Washington to far Japan
They honour noble Sharkey-san.

To Muscovites he is the Czar,
The vodka and the caviar.

Ned Kelly to the crowd down under,
To Danes the Thor of strength and thunder.

From Inishowen to Dublin 4,
From Strasbourg to the Sicily shore

His hospitality and gumption,
His ability to judge and function

And hold his own in all encounters
with poets, politicians, punters

Is legendary. We're proud of him.
He does us proud. Here's to you, Jim.

When James Sharkey was awarded his Alumnus Illustrissimus at St. Columb's, he discovered that Tony Doherty was present at the reception and rushed to have his photograph taken with him and Brady. Tony Doherty was one of the members of the St. Columb's side to win the GAA All-Ireland, the Hogan Cup, in 1965 (the only time St. Columb's ever won). Sharkey said that 'this is the man we need to honour'.

What comes out strongest in this interview is the 'show me the boy and I'll give you the man' aspect of the tough Catholic education of this era. Sharkey was one who took the best of this and managed to neutralise in his own mind the astringencies of St. Columb's. A near contemporary of Sharkey's once told me:

'St. Columb's gave me a discipline. It gave me a hardness. It taught me to be the best you can be. St. Columb's was the making of me. Without the 1947 Education Act, I would not have had a hope in hell of going to St. Columb's. There would have been two reasons: firstly, the aspiration would not have been engendered in the community and, secondly, economics. We did not understand the chance that 1947 gave us. I have had a confidence all my life and it came from going to St. Columb's.'

Sharkey saw a lot of brutality at his primary school – much more than in St. Columb's. Doubtless things had mollified by the time he entered the college. 'The Doker' [Derry: the strap] was used more sparingly. As he moved towards Senior, the Doker disappeared altogether.

Some of the most infamous teachers had gone from St. Columb's by this time. By then, a university style tutor/student relationship had developed and this is what Sharkey remembers best.

MF: Where were you born, James?

JS: I was born on 25 Lecky Road, which was right in the heart of what is now called the Bogside. (A historian of the nineteenth century and a defender of the Irish, Lecky wrote a history of Ireland in the eighteenth century which was a sort of vindication, at least from a unionist point of view, of the achievement of the Irish people.) Lecky Road was in a fairly poor and run-down part of Derry. After that we moved uphill to a more salubrious environment. My grandmother was very good – trained all her children, gave them some sort of trade to get on with.

My father had a job, he was in the merchant navy, and of course during the thirties he'd been mostly unemployed. He was a radio officer, a wireless operator as it was called, but during the thirties, there were no jobs. There was a recession, many ships were tied up. So the good news was he got a job in 1939. The bad news was that the war had just broken out. We moved from the Lecky Road to the Marlborough area of Derry. Lecky Road in 1949 would have been almost exclusively a Catholic community, whereas once you moved up the hill a bit, it was a much more mixed community. I grew up in a mixed community. My friends were both Catholics and Protestants.

MF: Your mother was from Donegal. Can you describe her area?

JS: My mother came from a very poor part of Donegal, very remote part of North Inishowen, called Urris. Her people were small farmers and fishermen. That was a magical place, an escape from Derry. I went down there as often as possible. To escape into really – what in reflection was for me – highly romanticised, and romanticised through the eyes of a young kid, a wonderland beside the sea, between the mountains, heather, sky and sun for ever. And I was lucky, because I saw an aspect of Ireland which had virtually disappeared everywhere else. It was in practice an English-speaking area, but the vocabulary was still maybe 50 per cent Irish, the structure of sentences was Irish, the names of all the places were in Irish, the names of all the fish were in Irish, the names of all the seaweeds were in Irish. The names of everything you did to cart a horse, to straddle a donkey and tether a sheep, that was all in Irish. Almost everybody I grew up with had a relative on the other side of the border in Inishowen. So I used to say that Derry and Glasgow were really both suburban developments of Inishowen. Derry and Inishowen are umbilically and inseparably connected.

MF: So are you Derry or Donegal?

JS: When it comes to a football match, Donegal versus Derry, I think I would probably go for Derry.

MF: Where did you go to primary school?

JS: I went to a Christian Brothers school in Derry called the Brow of the Hill, which was an extremely tough school, and gave me all of my sense of resistance against educational imposition.

MF: In what ways, if any, did the border impinge on your daily lives?

JS: My family would not have been aware of a political border. We were undoubtedly aware of a customs border. In the 1940s, everybody in Derry learned the art of taking things across the border, both on the Donegal side, where there was no tea, and on the Derry side, where there was no butter. That customs border, I think, probably continued one way or another up until the Common Market, which was 1972/73. But the concept of a political border imposed really very little.

MF: And the security forces – did they impinge on you?

JS: We grew up with a dread of these guys who were called B Specials. Certainly they were part of our psychological baggage. There was even a fellow who lived close to me in Marlborough Road who was a B Special and he used to run to evening duty; you could hear him running down past our house at 6.30 in the evening with his rifle on his shoulder, saying, 'hello Mrs Sharkey, hello Mrs Doherty', all that sort of thing. I don't want to trivialise it because it had a blacker side, there's no question, certainly from the perspective of somebody in the minority. The way we came to perceive the security apparatus was generally negative, because they were beyond us, outside of us, estranged from us, designed not to protect us but to protect something else. If there was an incident in Derry, you were involved in huge disarray and disturbance at the border. Then there would be queues going back for a long time.

MF: Did the Troubles create more of a divide between Donegal and Derry – the North and South?

JS: The Troubles had some strange negative psychological resonances which are now correcting themselves, I believe. Buncrana people and Derry people would have felt very close. Once the Troubles started – particularly sectarian assassinations – there was a wariness. People were more reluctant to cross the border, and sometimes rather than driving to Dublin through Derry they would take the long way around. Seamus Heaney often refers to the feeling that one had in moving through a checkpoint. If one was a unionist you felt a sense of confidence and of assurance and identification in moving through one of these checkpoints. If you were someone who you might say was from a nationalist tradition – the order to turn off your lights, the soldiers or the UDR men with the blackened faces – there was no way in which you were relaxed in those circumstances.

MF: What are your memories of the RUC as you were growing up?

JS: In Lecky Road there was a police barracks, and there was a police barracks in Rosemount. So right in the heart of the Bogside there was a very substantial station, which would have been an RIC station before it was an RUC station. You knew that the local policemen carried revolvers, but if they were the enemy, quote unquote, it was because they would chase you playing football in the streets. We weren't nervous then about going into a police station. I remember when we went out for a walk as kids, we once found something that looked like a Colorado beetle, during a period when there was a great Colorado beetle scare. There was a reward of £20 for anybody who could bring in a Colorado beetle, so off we went into Rosemount barracks with this little matchbox and the beetle inside, trying to get our £20. But it was only a class of a ladybird, at least that's what the cops told us.

MF: Do you remember political unrest in the Derry of your youth?

JS: As a kid I remember my mother being very determined that I shouldn't go to a St. Patrick's Parade in Derry in the 1950s. It was a parade where they were carrying a Tricolour. Eddie McAteer, who was the local Nationalist MP, was leading it. It was batonned off the streets. I assume without knowing it, but I'm sure if I researched it it would be true, that the policemen who were brought in to do the job of breaking up that particular parade would not have been from Derry. They would not have been your local cops.

And on 5th October 1968, the famous and decisive, indeed destiny-changing event, I remember at that march people speaking about the

Coleraine police and the Portrush police. In fact it was the specially recruited and trained riot police, wearing huge big heavy raincoats and shields and things that looked like motorcycle helmets. You can say that that would have been true for almost any police force. The way they manage local communities is very much influenced by the whole tradition of communitarian policing. The way they manage potentially riotous situations would have been handled quite differently.

MF: Can you describe your coming to take the Eleven Plus examination?

JS: The Christian Brothers School in Derry, in the North of Ireland, was interesting, because not many of the religious orders which you found in the Republic were allowed to teach in the northern half of Ireland, and the principal exception to that was the Christian Brothers. In leaving the Christian Brothers School I did, in this hall [Sharkey was interviewed in St. Columb's Hall], a competition in Irish history, and I won the gold medal for Irish history at the age of about ten. The day that the inspector came to our fifth class at the Christian Brothers – I was the one who put up his hand all the time – and I won a fountain pen as the star student who relieved the Brother of the great pressure of facing the inspector from the Stormont Government who was going to write a report.

The Christian Brothers Primary was a preparation for grammar school. They focused you on examinations, on the Eleven Plus. You went in on Saturday and you practiced with your IQ tests, because IQ tests were part of the Eleven Plus qualifying examination. If you were in the top stream of the Christian Brothers Primary, your chances of passing the Eleven Plus were certainly 70 out of 100. Learning to take one's punishment at the Christian Brothers, one got toughened.

MF: And then you passed. Do you remember that happening?

JS: The determining moment came when the post arrived, and it was part of the lore of everyone who was getting ready for life at the great, mature age of eleven or ten sometimes. A thick envelope meant you had passed the qualifying examination. Learned priests and learned professors all could pave a golden way to university, to training college, to a career as a teacher or as a priest, something beyond belief of many people. The thin envelope had a simple letter inside which said, 'Dear Mr and Mrs Sharkey, I'm sorry to tell you that your son has on this occasion been unsuccessful'. Now that was heartbreaking for many mothers, and many fathers, I'm sure.

MF: What was the St. Columb's that you found like?

JS: We were ten/eleven. You had to buy your blazer, and you were a college boy wearing your blazer. You walked up proud as punch with your blazer and your lovely crest, and everybody knew that you were a successful St. Columb's boy, destined forever for the great things in life. Little did they know what went on in some of the classrooms.

One accepted that corporal punishment from a Christian Brother or a lay teacher might be part of the normal course of things. The priest, within the psychology and the sociology and the structure of society in Derry, was somebody whom you were accustomed to regard as looking after your welfare. To encounter priests in a very obviously engaged educational role, with a tradition of strict discipline, was quite a profound eye-opener for many of the young guys: fellows from nice little two teacher or three teacher national schools, comfy schools, encountering this great trauma of teachers and priests who were extremely intelligent, probably the brightest of their generation, and yet who were determined on the basis of the doctrine of original sin, that you would either succeed or suffer the consequences.

MF: And there was streaming?

JS: There were four grades in my year, A, B, C and D. D was the top one; A, as we called it, was the lowest one. I ended up in A. And from that moment in time, my life at St. Columb's was easy for ever. Everything was simple, and I was under no particular pressure. I could avoid homework, which was the most important thing in my life in those days. That was my first experience of streaming.

We all knew that we were in 2A. We were the lowest of the low in the pecking order of that particular year, and we developed a culture, a culture that stayed with me for a lot of my life, what I call the culture of the three Ss. Anybody who studied at night was called a 'stew', anybody

who told on another boy was called a 'squeak', and anybody who tried to sit in the front seat of the class and talk up to the master was called a 'suck'. So you had a stew, a squeak and a suck. In 2A, nobody could be a stew, a squeak or a suck. We knew that up in the higher classes they were all stews, they were all squeaks and they were all sucks. You could never depend on them to save your bacon. We had a strict code of omerta, and we survived.

MF: To what extent do you think St. Columb's formed your mind?

JS: I think that the ethos of the city, the ethos of the streets, influenced me as much as my first three years in St. Columb's. Survival in the first three years leading up to the Junior Certificate was key. Those final senior years, those two senior years, were really a preparation for something extraordinary. That is, I think, where St. Columb's came into its own. This was what in those days were called the advanced level period or phase. No matter how much you were a rebel and rejected education, you were always aware that there were teachers of a certain sophistication with whom you empathised. You encountered these people as I did for the subjects which were of keen interest to me.

That interconnection, that reassociation, that profound engagement with them intellectually was a transformative engagement, and for me it was very important. I learned then to ask the question, 'why?' I owe those people a special debt of gratitude.

MF: How would you describe the sort of education you got?

JS: We were beneficiaries of the Beveridge system. Our curriculum was determined in Belfast, and the curriculum by and large was a curriculum not unlike the curriculum which would have been established also in Britain. So we had a sense of the British imperial tradition. This was before the period of British self-doubt in the fifties and in the sixties. It began to change perhaps with the Labour government and decolonisation. We certainly, in our history studies, had a sense of Britain's contribution to the world. Of course, we were skeptical about it. But, importantly, we also had substantial engagement with the Gaelic tradition. This was something quite unusual, and in the unionist tradition they wouldn't have had this engagement. We had it from a historical perspective (that is, the long view of Irish history) and also in terms of the great resurgence of Irish literature, sometimes called 'the Hidden Ireland' of Munster or, more recently, 'the Hidden Ulster', the poets of the eighteenth century. St. Columb's was one of the most important defenders of the northern tradition in Irish, in the language, in its validity, in its dialects.

When I went to UCD I was never sure that my contemporaries from Dublin and from the South-West were as conscious of the northern Gaelic tradition as we were of their southern Gaelic tradition. And they certainly did not have the same familiarity with the British experience.

I have no inhibition about being called an Ulsterman. When I met Dr. Paisley I called myself an Ulsterman. Whether he accepted me as an Ulsterman, I don't know.

MF: Why did you go to UCD rather than Queen's?

JS: Our English teacher, S.B. O'Kelly, had been educated at UCD. His university environment of preference was University College Dublin. Our history teacher had a sense of Dublin being a capital city. So that was certainly an important point of influence. It influenced seven, eight, nine of us, and we all went off to Dublin that year.

A number of very brilliant graduates of St. Columb's College had gone to Queen's and were already becoming celebrities and stars. Coulter had founded the Glee Club, and Eamonn McCann was the champion of the political and debating literati. There was, quote unquote, a taint of socialism around all of this. Certainly within the influences which we confronted, that would have been a subliminal element. I never regret going to Dublin.

But every so often, maybe once a month, sometimes less, you would thumb up to Derry, and do 150 miles. There is an intimacy about Derry, and there's a spirit of egalitarianism about Derry. We all went to play snooker in Cnoc na Ross and that was very important for all of us. When it came to courting girls, there was no class distinction. You went to the Corinthian to rock and roll or you went to the Lady of Lourdes Hall for *Ceilidh* music on a Saturday night. Some of our heroes were the most extraordinary characters. Only if you come from Derry do you understand the expression, to be 'the fastest boot in Derry'.

In those days I knew almost everybody. It was a city of 56,000 people. Away from Derry you felt a sense of loss, and I felt that sense of loss strongly all of my life. I remember often taking my kids from Dublin, driving up. There's a place just after Magheramason, you move on towards Newbuildings, and there's a great sweep of the Foyle. Suddenly a huge, panoramic, magnificent vista breaks before you. You can see St. Columb's Cathedral, St Eugene's Cathedral, you can see Marlborough, and Oakfield and Rosemount, Creggan, the cemetery, all of that, in one miraculous manifestation, and one extraordinary moment of intense passion. The tears are almost in your eyes at that moment, and there I am again and again and again, trying to explain to my kids that this is the greatest city in the world. At a certain stage after you'd left Strabane, you began more and more to sing Phil Coulter's song, 'The Town I Loved So Well'.

MF: You were a teacher at St. Columb's for a spell?

JS: I got a job teaching, a luxurious job. People were muttering in the background, 'why has he done this surrender, betrayal?' I got a job teaching in St. Columb's College, but teaching a subject I love, history. I had already been studying Russian Studies in Birmingham. I had met my wife, who was Indian, she's from India. (We were one of the first so-called intercultural marriages in England. There was actually an article written about our marriage in the paper. We tried to keep it a great secret, but my poor wife's parents found out, when people showed them the article. Their beloved daughter had gone off and married what is called a *gori*, a white man.)

That was a momentous year to be teaching in Derry, '68/'69, quite an extraordinary year. One phenomenon in Derry when the Troubles broke out was that riots were suppressed in those days by a mixture of baton charge (I think this was before so-called baton rounds) and a thing called CS gas. My wife, who has been very important in my life, was asthmatic. She suffered very badly from CS gas. She had to spend nearly three weeks in the hospital in the Waterside. There was a chest hospital in that part of Derry, the Waterside.

Once that happened we knew that we couldn't stay in Derry. That was in the period after what historically came to be called 'The Battle of the Bogside'. I suppose the decisive, the existential moment was when we returned to Derry shortly after we had got married. It's an interesting thing, again it relates to the psychology of Derry, and to the great debate about the 'Eleven Plus Generation', what they represented: I often thought that tragically a failure of unionism was the inability to absorb that generation. The civil rights movement began (naturally, first and foremost with the search for civil rights, civil liberties) with representatives of that generation who had achieved both the qualifying examination and the benefits of a grammar school education, and ultimately a university or third level education. We sought equality, influenced as we were by the rhetoric, the passion, the intensity and the scale of the American civil rights movement, by the leadership of the American black civil rights movement. We wanted all of our community to prosper. Remember that around that time one of the great employers of the male Catholic population in Derry had closed down. I can't remember the exact year but around 1966 or 1967, the BSR (Birmingham Sound Reproduction) closed. There was a terrible shortage of housing. So it was important for us that if we were to move ahead, our community should be able to move ahead with us. We were conscious also of the need to engage in politics in a way which was novel, and not to make mistakes. Certainly, as someone who had studied history, that was important for me. I was also aware of the need to avoid anything that might be seen as sectarian.

MF: So October 5th, 1968 happened. What do you remember of that day?

JS: We had heard about a march that was planned on the 5th of October, so we decided to walk over the bridge to the march. Just as we turned the corner, we noticed that television cameras were there and we saw Gerry Fitt getting hit on the head with a truncheon. He put his hand up, and it was bloody, and he showed it to the TV camera. There were speeches. Eamonn McCann made a speech. Students from Queen's were caught between two lines of police. Suddenly, unexpectedly, the fire ignited. How it ignited, you can debate. The police, being riot police, went to town. They batonned right, left and centre. I saw some people whom I knew getting badly beaten. I decided to walk straight for the line of policemen, and for whatever reason, maybe because I was wearing a good suit, I only got the touch of a baton. But it was a decisive moment, because the television cameras were there. A major journalist such as Mary Holland from *The Observer* had been featuring Derry, and she was there. This was not a backstreet semi-visible, opaque event. This was now a front line, front page, world-leading evening news story.

For Eamonn McCann, people in the Derry Housing Action Committee – for all of them, something happened I think which they could never have imagined. Northern Ireland was never, never the same again. The curtains came down on those small communities, on those elements of reconciliation, of middle class camaraderie between Catholic and Protestant. The Troubles permanently began. I think that the 5th of October march was one of the two destiny-shaping moments in contemporary Irish history, because the whole phase of thirty-five years of trouble followed on after that, and the rapid deterioration in Anglo-Irish relations, deterioration in community relations. The other moment which shaped modern Ireland of course was

joining the European Union, joining as it was the Common Market (the EEC) in 1973.

MF: Protest continued over the next few years leading up to Bloody Sunday?

JS: I thought that the contribution of Martin Luther King – 'an eye for an eye leaves everyone blind' – was also the contribution of John Hume. He had become a philosopher of non-violence. The tradition of non-violence and civil disobedience had profound and very impressive origins, not just in the eighteenth century but more recently in the literature of Tolstoy and I had studied Russian history. And of course in the role of Gandhi.

I continued to believe in the philosophy of non-violence, and I believe that it had a regenerative and redemptive significance. I went to Derry as I say, regularly, and I was there on one Sunday, the 30th of January 1972. I was at home and the young guy next door told me that there was an anti-internment march happening in Creggan that day. Both my two brothers were going to that march, so we all set off together. We thought of it as a reconstruction of the civil rights marches that we had known in the year 1968. There was a feeling of carnival joy – people telling jokes.

We noticed that there were lots of soldiers on the top of buildings. There was an element of tension in the air. Bernadette Devlin spoke, and I suppose we all got ready to go home, when suddenly we heard zoom, zoom, zoom. We knew that these were bullets, high velocity bullets being fired. We assumed that that's what it was – a sort of warning, head off, get away.

But within five minutes we began to hear stories that others had not got away, and had got cornered, and that many people had died. It was a traumatic moment. Although I was very, very much there in a personal capacity, it taught me that one couldn't easily take people onto the streets again; that non-violence had probably reached its limit and civil disobedience certainly had reached its ultimate moment, tragically, on that particular day.

The tragedy of the Troubles was that there were two competing perspectives. I remember driving over to the [largely Protestant] Waterside, looking for petrol because I was going back to Donegal that evening. It was clear that the way the young man in the petrol station felt about the events of the day was quite different from the way that I felt. Reconciliation became a very, very fundamental drive in my personality, to try and bring the two communities to a closer view of their own identity, their own place in Northern Ireland, their own place in Ireland, and their own grievances. Even on the 5th of October I remember having a debate with someone. I said, 'I wonder how many unionists, how many working class Protestants are here today?' I felt that maybe things were just a little bit too early, because if you got off on the wrong foot you could be seen as sectarian. The great success of John Hume, I would argue, has been his persistent focus on the concept of reconciliation.

MF: And as a diplomat, how did the events you witnessed at home impact, say, in America?

JS: Washington was certainly in those days the centre of the world. It was the most important capital in the world. Moscow was very important, where I had also served. There was a British perspective in presenting the Northern Ireland issue, in which they were honest brokers within a difficult situation of competing tribes. That analysis of Northern Ireland I found terribly offensive. The Reagan administration had a very strong focus on what was called the international terrorism network.

This was a terrorism network which had its centre in Moscow. From an Irish-American point of view there was an absolute need to liberate Irish American engagement in Ireland from any kind of association with violence or terrorism. From the point of view of Irish America there was a credibility and impact. Mrs Thatcher had rejected the New Ireland Forum Report [1984] with her famous 'out, out, out'. But, against that, the first ever resolution passed by both Senate and House on the Irish 'Troubles' was one endorsing the New Ireland Forum. And later Reagan endorsed the Forum. That was the scope of the change that occurred in America.

A Conversation with James Sharkey
Eamonn McCann, Paul Brady and
Phil Coulter

In this inter-chapter James Sharkey leads an interesting conversation with three of the film's participants on the subject of their education and its uniqueness. The argument that the hierarchical structure of the Orange State limited the oppourtunities of working class Protestants in a way that was not true of working class Catholics is a key point. The Squirarchy, so-called, maintained the Orange machine for as long as they could — which explains a lot of the archaic make-up of the North until the 1960s — because it was in the interests of their property franchise and rigged voting system.

PC: According to David Ervine, Protestant boys could leave school at thirteen or fourteen and walk into the shipyard. Or the girls could work in the linen plants ...

EM: The lack of educational advancement of Protestant working class kids, particularly of Protestant working class boys, is absolutely striking and shocking in Northern Ireland at the minute. One of the differences between being from the Shankill [Protestant working class area in Belfast] and being from the Bogside I think was this – that the Protestant community was much more class structured. There was that whole layer of bowler-hatted, respectable upper working-class and the great manufacturers at the top. I think people got the sense of being looked down on by their own in a way that we never had, because there was nobody to look down on us. I think it has done lasting damage.

JS: The essential thing about Derry was it was an egalitarian society. It didn't tolerate snobbery.

PC: How did it feel returning today?

EM: I never felt at home here, ever. I was surprised at how little I felt, because I'd been wondering what would I feel when I saw the classrooms. I felt remarkably little. I found the religion in St. Columb's really oppressive: some aspects, at least, sort of what we were being taught was absolutely ridiculous. The idea that you (and they said it explicitly in so many words) could roast in hell forever for masturbating.

PC: Is that not true?

JS: The crucial element was whether (and how) you interacted with particular teachers. If you were unlucky it was a disaster. We don't have to mention names ...

EM: You can identify them as Moses, the Bird, Big Fla, the Doc: there was a quartet you didn't want to meet on a dark night. The Monk, you didn't want to meet him.

JS: I used to get twelve dokes a day here.

PC: Twelve dokes a day! We were softies. You were the hard chaws. The Rosemount boys.

JS: It made us hard men. There are two aspects of St. Columb's which are important. First thing is we received an education which offered a view of the world which is quite unique in Ireland and Britain, because we were able to connect with the whole Gaelic tradition and heritage. I don't mean it in the sense of a Gaelic nationalism. I mean with touching 'the Hidden Ulster', all of this sort of thing – which of course they had in the South. But we'd something that they didn't have in the South. We were part of the British educational system, so we had a view of the British tradition in the world, the imperial grandeur. We took it with a pinch of salt, and some of our teachers scored out particular lines of history books ...

EM: The name McCauley comes to mind. This English allegation that 'Charles Stuart Parnell and Kitty O'Shea were anything more than good friends'. I might be entirely wrong with this, I think that's one of the explanations for the achievement of Heaney, Deane and so on – there was a clash that then became creative. There was tension – there were two worlds there. Even more than two worlds, all in collision I think at that particular time. It wasn't so much a confluence of different cultures; they were crashing into one another and something emerged from that.

JS: We had a profound sense of global history in the sense that for a long time – Britain was a dominant global power. So we were introduced to the civilisation not simply of the white Commonwealth, but also places like India and China. Also, the English teacher and the history teacher really captured my imagination.

EM: Is that Squeak O'Kelly, yeah?

JS: Squeak, yeah. I was called a budding boy who hadn't bloomed yet.

PC: A late developer?

JS: No, because I'd no interest in developing. You were going to succeed against the odds. Derry is a city of gamblers, the Irish are a race of gamblers. We all enjoyed betting, but it gave you a chance to bet against the odds.

EM: When you left school at twenty past three, I'm not saying that you denied being at St. Columb's, but you dropped off St. Columb's, because you had to do that.

PB: It's only now that I'm coming back here I realise that St. Columb's and the city were inextricably entwined.

JS: I've known you now for quite a while, but suddenly I see you in terms of the boarding community, also as a separate spirit.

PB: Returning here, I didn't feel very much, as Eamonn said earlier. But I was surprised at how little things have changed. First thing I did was look up at the second window on the left, on the third floor of the right hand building to see where I had spent three years in a bedroom up there. And when I went up to have a secret look at it, I found it's been turned into a recording studio. I felt worse yesterday when I was marshalling my thoughts about it. When I got here today actually I didn't feel an awful lot.

JS: There is a process of exorcising, removing things, I don't know, sentiments, feelings. Although we in some ways were not admitting these feelings, it was obviously an intense period, a period of intense friendships, a period of intense experience.

EM: In a funny way the main thing that I got out of St. Columb's actually was religion. The chapel was the only place that had any effect on me when I walked down to it – partly because it's hardly changed at all. We were lectured and, as is the case with all religion, we were enclosed there. The religion was taught with a sort of dogmatic certainty. You weren't allowed to question anything. It also gave me a real interest in religion, because I was really interested in the process and question and argument. Really, I used to know about the Council of Trent, the Synod of Whitby and stuff like that.

JS: I never took it as seriously as you, obviously in terms of your own personality – there was a striving for knowledge or a challenging of the system. The system failed, I would argue, if it wasn't able to incorporate your questioning.

EM: My conclusion was that it couldn't incorporate my questioning because it was untrue, because there was no substance to it.

JS: That was a huge conclusion to take.

EM: I did Greek – Aeschylus, Sophocles. I'm really pleased I learnt it. One of the reasons so many people remember Squeak O'Kelly: he allowed you to question. He was the English teacher. Looking back on weird experiments, I remember a boy named Pat who sat beside me. We were doing *Macbeth* and Pat suggested that since it was set in Scotland that perhaps Shakespeare had intended that it would be done in a Scottish accent. I remember him saying in a Scottish accent, 'Tomorrow and tomorrow and tomorrow/Creeps in this petty pace from day to day ...' and Squeak let him go on like that and we discussed it and so forth. Now where else in St. Columb's could you bring up an almost jocose point, and be allowed to run with it?

Paul Brady

Paul Brady recalls his first being aware of the difference in the people across the Sperrin Mountains when he first went to St. Columb's – which drew its student population from all over the province. He had never heard the Scottish-sounding accents of 'the other side of the mountains' until he entered grammar school. Brady points to the Sperrin Mountains as a major landmark and a separating force between Tyrone and south Derry. Likewise, the people he met in Lifford, Co. Donegal, where his father cycled to work, were different in their accents and political backgrounds. Ironically, Brady's parents had settled on the border to limit its effect on their lives, to make the border not part of their lives. Living in Strabane, west Tyrone, the 12ths (the 12th of July commemorates the Protestant victory at the Battle of the

166

Boyne; the 12th of August celebrates the Protestant triumph at the Siege of Derry) were strictly observed: businesses closed and gloom descended on the area, from a Catholic's point of view. During the triumphal Orange marches of July and August, the Brady family went to Bundoran. His mother was Vice-Principal in a Quaker primary school in Strabane. Brady went there himself and found it quite free from prejudice. But there were sectarian undercurrents of which he was unaware at that age: the principal was a Protestant and Brady's mother was a Catholic. His mother always harboured the suspicion that she did not get a principalship because she was a Catholic. Brady's mother's religion, the likely reason for her lack of promotion to principalship, would scarcely have happened at Heaney's school. While Heaney's Anahorish school was mixed both in terms of gender and religion, more importantly it was under Catholic management. Nonetheless, Brady encountered at his primary school the ease with which two traditions could be intertwined. Both of these traditions came through in his music when he first started playing songs in a hotel in Donegal during school summers.

Moving from the relatively free-thinking atmosphere of his Quaker primary school to St. Columb's was a stunning surprise for Brady. The St. Columb's boys seemed hard-line Republicans to Brady. They also came from all over Ulster: Derry, Tyrone, Antrim, Donegal and some came from Fermanagh. It took a long time to get used to being there and he feels that St. Columb's fostered little that is good or instinctive in him.

Just over twenty priests taught in St. Columb's during this period. Most of them had not been asked if they wanted to be posted there, resulting in a great deal of misplacement. One mathematician, for example, was assigned to teach Ancient Greek. Priests were paid one hundred pounds a year which worked out at scarcely 25 per cent or so of their net salary. The rest of their salary funded the college. This surely fed the resentment that some of them felt towards the boys; it also helps to explain the baronial attitude of some priests. Priests could be snotty and scathing about boys from the city. They disliked the working class rising. Others were more humane. One maths teacher was gentle. He would ask the boys if they understood. Incomprehension in other classes was a mandate for a beating. If there was clerical influence in the family, then they would push the boy to go to St. Columb's.

While the Catholic middle class sneered at the new generation from the Bogside coming through, the imbalance did not take long to correct itself. Relative to Protestant intransigence, social climbing in the Catholic community was easily accomplished. Brady is right when he says that Catholics were on their way up and 'fighting hard'.

When Brady mentions 'manly stuff', St. Columb's' brand of masculinity, he comes close to one of the most problematic impositions for some students at the school. Brady suggests that the rigid view of what a man is, as expounded by St. Columb's, was tendentious and damaging. They wanted you to become a man, but what kind of a man? One who is more warped than shaped? Choice did not much enter the life of a boy aged eleven during this period. Boarding school had the effect of retarding many people's development rather than preparing them for the life beyond. They were precluded from making decisions, which is hardly adult. Students who emerged from St. Columb's were often in their late twenties before they came into their own. It could be argued that Catholic education in the North was peculiar because it was at once a jail sentence (youth spent in extremis) and a jail break (the advent of their asserting full participation for Catholics in the North).

Brady has very few fond memories of St. Columb's, but he was popular among some seniors. They used to ask him to play piano on rainy Saturday afternoons. Brady enjoyed it too. The imposing building was grey inside and out with few entertainment outlets. As one student recalls, returning to the boarding school after holidays, 'I remembered the sick feeling in my stomach, as I traveled towards the school after holidays and saw the river and then the bridge and then the school itself appear, and got ready for the click of hobnailed boots in corridors and the smell of chalk and carbolic soap, and the clatter of crockery as the first vile evening meal was served'. Priests had a little room opposite the student refectory where they ate.

Father McCauley used to tell boarders that they were solid stock (in contrast to papier-mâché day-boys). His theorising built like silt and they began to believe it. Brady, unlike other boarders, speaks of 'not being the thing' in St. Columb's, not fitting. It is true that his profile does seem like that of a misbegotten day-boy. It is easy to imagine his being happier if he returned home every evening on the Strabane bus, playing guitar at home and so forth. Playing the latest hits on guitar would, during a turbulent adolescence, surely have been cathartic. Brady did all he could to improve his situation but the school ethos was too stringent during this era to accommodate his needs. It is apparent in several instances during this interview that the system failed him. The boys paced the walks up and down in front of the college. They had a clique of friends or sometimes just one or two friends. But it was very lonely. At night in the dormitory they felt abandoned, farmed out to boarding school. Wains cried and some tried to run away.

Brady speaks of how 'the ducking' experienced by many of the first year boys, 'the yaps', revealed itself to be more brutal than expected. Ducking was an initiation rite. While the act seemed harmless enough, the fact that deans let it happen felt sinister. Similarly, the dean actually cultivated snow-ball fights between the seniors and juniors. It started off innocuously enough with long-range shots but soon descended into gangs of seniors picking on a junior, rounding him up like game and shoving snow down his shirt, together with a few slaps.

One teacher remembers Brady as a very kind boy who sang one year in the school play. The teacher also remembers McCann as a quiet boy who played violin in school concerts. Coulter was bright and lithe, an obvious choice for Ariel in *The Tempest*. Heaney played the lead in a play one year later.

Memory fiddles with things and Brady acknowledges that some of his recollections of St. Columb's may be unreliable. To him, a number of St. Columb's boys were quite nationalist, but there was a mix as there would be in any population. Parents' opinions continued down the line. No one political slant was prevalent. Occasional remarks showed a certain resentment but most teachers seldom mentioned nationalism. Brady found hardened Republicans in the school, but they had been

cast in that mould before they arrived in St. Columb's. One teacher used to get students to scratch out the 'we' and 'us' in history textbooks that referred to British history. Students mocked this teacher for his pedantry. Other teachers, such as Hume who taught Brady French, were much more liberal.

Many students were seduced by the political leanings of St. Columb's and they identified themselves according to distinct political backgrounds when they came of age.

As is apparent in this interview, Brady learned from St. Columb's that he is on his own and either he embraces that and cultivates it in his music or he is a nobody. Some of those who became politicised as a result of the civil rights movement would say the opposite: that either they are loyal to the community and serve it or they are irredeemably lost.

In 1963, a small group from St. Columb's went to UCD. By the following year, twenty or thirty students enrolled there. A reasonably good Senior Certificate earned a university scholarship. The scholarship they won at the end of their schooling obtained for any university on the island of Ireland. Sharkey and Brady were flatmates in UCD during their second year, together with another St. Columb's student, Willie Melaugh. They led a sheltered existence. Brady was remarkable among the St. Columb's boys in UCD in that he mixed outside the Derry circle which, incidentally, accords with Newman's idea of a university – to open out. There was a radiator at the entrance of Earlsfort Terrace where the Derry boys would gather. They were contemptuous of the Dublin intelligentsia who ran the L and H Debating Society. Sinead Cusack, Anthony Clare, Ruth Dudley Edwards, Patrick Cosgrove, Vincent Browne (head of Young Fine Gael) and Henry Kelly were at UCD at this time.

Artists who come through often have a belief in themselves and an idea of what they want to do. They take the blows and their determination brings them forward. St. Columb's was, it seems from this interview, a good preparation for the brutality of the music industry.

The first song reproduced here is a direct recollection of Brady's Latin classes in St. Columb's. The second, 'Nobody Knows', echoes a mood and comment he expresses in his interview.

The World Is What You Make It

I knew this African called Hannibal
Rock it, roll it, send it down the avenue
Went out to see the Roman Empire fall
Uh huh? Uh huh?
Two thousand elephants in gold chain mail
Take it, shake it, make it what you wanna be
Them Roman legionnaires they hit the trail
Uh huh?

The world is what you make it
The world is what you make it, Baby
The world is what you make it

When Cleopatra ruled in Egypt's land
Jump down, turn around, look at what the monkey did
She went to find herself a mighty man
Uh huh? Uh huh?
In come Antonio from Italy
Haul it, ball it, drag it up the pyramid
He never knew how hot a girl could be
Uh huh?

The world is what you make it
The world is what you make it, Baby
The world is what you make it

Don't start to hit me with your 'no can do'
Bluesin', losin', workin' up an attitude
Clean up them windows, let the sun shine through
Uh huh? Uh huh?
There ain't no happy time without no pain
Heartbreak, new date, move on up the alleyway
Pick up them pieces, hit the road again
Uh huh?

The world is what you make it
The world is what you make it, Baby
The world is what you make it

Nobody Knows

Johnny's got high expectations
He's gonna rise
Everyone knows that Johnny is ready
He's ready to fly
Up on the rooftop he turns to the crowd
No one is waiting
No one is there

Nobody knows why Elvis threw it all away
Nobody knows what Ruby had to hide
Nobody knows why some of us get broken hearts
And some of us find a world that's clear and bright
You could be packed up and ready
Knowing exactly where to go
How come you miss the connection?

No use in asking ... the answer is nobody knows
No use in asking ... the answer is nobody knows

Johnny will keep his illusions
What else can he do?
You can pretend that it would be different
If it happened to you

But up on the rooftop, it's a whole other world
And who could see heaven
And not want to stay?

Nobody knows why Elvis threw it all away
Nobody knows what Ruby had to hide
Nobody knows why some of us get broken hearts
And some of us find a world that's clear and bright
You could be packed up and ready
Knowing exactly where to go
How come you miss the connection?

No use in asking ... the answer is nobody knows
No use in asking ... the answer is nobody knows

MF: Can you say a little about your background and where you are from?

PB: Both of my parents were primary school teachers. My mother was trained in the North under the British system. My father was trained in the South. They both wanted to work after they were married, so they wanted to find some place to live where he could teach in the South and she could teach in the North, so Strabane/Lifford was where they settled. He taught across the border, across the bridge in the Republic, and my mother taught in Sion Mills, a village three miles south of Strabane.

MF: You had an atypical primary education. Can you elaborate a little on that?

PB: I went to my mother's school where I had my primary education in the British education system. I went to school with my mother every day. I didn't realise it until later, but Sion Mills primary school was a very unusual school in Northern Ireland or anywhere in Ireland for that matter, in that it was both mixed sex and mixed religion. The ethos in which the school was set up was egalitarian. Somewhere in the mid-nineteenth century a family called the Herdmans opened a linen mill in Sion Mills, which became one of the biggest mills in the UK at the time. There was some Quaker aspect to the Herdmans, so they had a kind of an egalitarian outlook. They didn't want to have any exclusion at all in the school. I was educated in the school with Catholics, Protestants, boys and girls, from the age of four until I was ten. That was a fundamental experience for me, which only very few people in Northern Ireland had, because most schools were segregated, both sex-wise and religion-wise.

My mother had a car, a Morris 8. She had the car and drove three miles to Sion Mills. My father cycled across the bridge into the Republic. His school was probably closer to our house as the crow flies than her school, although it was in a different country. That was an interesting part of growing up there: I had a dual nationality, dual culture. For one reason or another, as I grew older, I began to feel more comfortable in the Republic, in Donegal.

MF: And how did you end up in St. Columb's?

PB: It probably was an obvious place to send me to school. It was in the same diocese. But why I actually went boarding, I never quite understood, and really still don't. Let's face it, I only lived fourteen miles away, and a large part of people from Strabane were taking the bus every day. There was a fashion going round at the time among parents who were interested in education, that sending your kids to boarding school would be more focusing, they would get better grades. They'd get a better education. I never quite got used to it. It was hard not to think that your parents were trying to get rid of you, which is probably a bit cruel. When you're that age and you go to a boarding school that's that close, you're thinking, 'what am I doing here?' I sat my mother and father down in later years and I asked, 'why did you send me boarding?' They kind of said, 'well because we wanted you to do well'. Oh, television, oh, it's going to be the death of us all. So get them away from it. Distractions. I couldn't quite understand it. I threw it into the basket of any kind of simmering nonsense that kids in their teens have about their parents.

MF: So you went from a fairly congenial primary school into an astringent boarding school. What are your first memories of St. Columb's?

PB: Shock, horror, awe, shock. I had no experience that was going to prepare me for going into a boarding school. Being in a monocultural, monosex kind of atmosphere was quite a shock to me, and it took me a long time to get accustomed to it. I didn't have any experience of other parts of Northern Ireland, say east of the Sperrin Mountains which is a whole different vibe altogether, with strange accents, which now I know only to be south Derry accents and Antrim accents. But at the time they might have been from Timbuktu to me.

MF: What was that culture? In what way was it a different vibe for you?

PB: I couldn't fathom their attitudes: the whole south Derry and west Antrim part of the college. They came from a part of Northern Ireland which I now know to have been very nationalist and very Republican and very into Gaelic culture – Gaelic football. Although my father came from County Sligo and he played Gaelic football and he spoke Irish because he taught Irish in school, still, it was a whole culture that I had never been exposed to before, and it was totally strange to me. Gaelic football? What's that? Handball? What's a handball alley? I never learned Irish until I went to St. Columb's. That's one of the things I'm actually grateful to St. Columb's for – it introduced me to Irish culture in a way that I hadn't been up to then. Strabane was a fairly tense environment in the 1950s, or the mid-1950s, as the IRA campaign had impinged quite strongly in Strabane, so there was a very strong British army and police and B Special vibe around the town. When the IRA thing happened in the sixties, all these British army vehicles came into Strabane. They were in camouflage from Cyprus, so they were all yellow coloured from those desert campaigns. There wasn't an atmosphere of resentment or political intrigue around my upbringing at all. When I went to St. Columb's, I suddenly realised that there were other things going on in the world that I didn't know, and it was very hard to deal with all that stuff initially.

MF: What else was hard to deal with at St. Columb's?

PB: The culture of violence – within two days of my arriving at the college as an eleven year old I had been beaten up three or four times. I had been forced and goaded into fighting with other boys. I had been taken out and given a ducking as they called it. Technically speaking, you were supposed to just have your head held under the outside tap of the school and get your head wet. But actually it was a very brutal experience. Priests would be walking around the Walks in the college, reading their breviaries and just totally ignoring all this. This was a ritual that happened to first years when we came into college. The second years, who'd got it the year before, decided it was culturally acceptable to initiate the first years with this regime of terror, which went on for 24, 48 hours. You were subjected to this unbelievable horror and terror. This was the ritual.

I certainly wasn't robust. I suppose I was a soft wee fellow. I wore glasses at the time, and I had never been in a fight in my life. I'd never hit anybody in my life. So suddenly you're being goaded into fighting somebody called Bobby Burns (I remember his name was Bobby Burns), some young fellow from South Derry was pitted against me, almost like two pit bulls. I didn't know who the fellow was, but somebody said something to somebody, and that was considered to be enough justification.

MF: What sort of background did St. Columb's want?

PB: The desirable background was an overtly nationalist background and that you were familiar with Gaelic culture. Strabane people were sort of not quite the thing, it seemed to me. These are just my emotional reactions to how I was perceived and treated in the school. If you were really good at Gaelic football, if you were great at running and sports, if you were really brilliant at maths or something, you tended to get noticed in St. Columb's. I wanted to keep my head down. I wanted to get through this.

MF: But you were good at music.

PB: The kind of musical ethos in St. Columb's didn't allow for the kind of talent that I subsequently seem to have had. It was more geared towards classical exams, classical music, certainly, and you were taught to play Beethoven and Mozart. I was never really interested in learning about musical theory. I was never really interested in playing the Moonlight Sonata. I was an instinctive musician. One year, they did the *Yeomen of the Guard* by Gilbert and Sullivan, and I had one of the main roles in it as a singer. Dame Carruthers I was. That was before my voice broke. What I really was interested in at the time was pop music. The first Christmas after I went to St. Columb's was Christmas 1958. My parents asked me whether I would like a guitar or a harmonica for Christmas. I just tossed a coin and I said a guitar. But I wasn't allowed to bring the guitar to St. Columb's with me. So for six years, as a boarder, I learned nothing on the guitar really. Why was I not allowed to bring a guitar to the college? They thought Elvis Presley – guitars are bad. Piano good, guitar bad. Bad juju.

That was really stupid. I do resent that. When I got home, I would listen to the radio. We weren't allowed to listen to the radio in the college. People had crystal sets. A crystal set is a little head, a little earphone. You can pick up the radio on it. And what I really liked was the Shadows, Chuck Berry, Little Richard, Jerry Lee Lewis, Elvis of course, Buddy Holly, and then the Beatles.

MF: Where exactly in the college did you board?

PB: I was in a cubicle for the first couple of years in St. Columb's. As you went through the ranks you got moved into rooms with two or three boys. It was an imposing building.

MF: Geographically, where is St. Columb's?

PB: You're driving up along the Strabane Road into Derry, you know, you can immediately see it up on the hill there, overlooking the river and then overlooking the Bogside on the other side.

MF: Did the priests in St. Columb's contribute to this notion of what way you should be?

PB: Priests come from a background of self-denial or being denied, and there are certain aspects of humanity that they're not allowed to engage with. So I think that somehow coloured how they thought young men should be.

There was certainly a kind of notion, collective notion in the college hierarchy, of a certain type of man you would grow up into. I felt like not getting noticed, so I kept my head down. It got me into the habit for six years of juking about the place. It is wrong for a child at that age to be feeling like that.

MF: What did St. Columb's give you on the positive side?

PB: What I learned from St. Columb's about myself was this outsider-ness that I perceived from those days and that has remained with me all the time since. Maybe I was always a bit of an outsider. I think in a way that's kind of what has been at the core of whatever artistry I have: the notion that, all right, you're on your own here pal. Whatever you think, nobody else really agrees with. You either run with that and love it, and nurture it and fight for it, or you walk away from everything and you become a nobody. That's what honed my artistry. I don't want to be co-

opted by anybody. It's a marketing disaster. In the world of commerce, what is Paul Brady? Nobody knows. I don't even know.

It's my mother in me who gave me that fight and push. It's very simple to say my father gave me my talent, my mother gave me my drive – nobody's going to put me down. My father was very easy going and loved to sing, loved to act. My mother was a strong person in many ways, and she felt she had to fight her corner. She was a Catholic teacher in a school which was, I suppose, largely Protestant, in the sense that the principal was always Protestant, never Catholic. There was always an element that you're slightly underclass here.

MF: And that rankled?

PB: Of course it rankled. That was the common experience in Northern Ireland. Anywhere there was discrimination at all it rankled.

MF: What good things did you learn and experience in St. Columb's?

PB: I really became good at Irish, and I really love the Irish language. I liked Latin. I loved geography. I'm only realising this now as I'm talking to you, I never really gave myself over to the St. Columb's experience. I might have actually made more of an impact if I had trusted more; I might have developed closer relationships with teachers, more mentoring situations. But for some reason, the minute I arrived there I felt oh-oh, this is not me. I stopped trying at a very early time. My own recollections of how I was perceived there may not be very trustworthy.

In the last year I ended up playing the college organ for Benediction and for Mass. I think Phil Coulter was the one who did it before me. They trusted me to go and play the organ for Benediction.

I hung round mostly with a fellow called Johnny Heffernan from Strabane. He was a loner too. We would spend most of the time just walking round together.

It was never a place that I was going to want to extend my relationship with after it was over. And I didn't really want to associate with people I'd met there after I left it because to do that would have constantly dragged me back into that whole memory.

I think Seamus Heaney liked St. Columb's because he came from that culture, east of the Sperrin Mountains, south Derry. That whole culture that he grew up in was what was liked in St. Columb's. That was the stuff to be.

MF: Manly?

PB: Manly. Exactly. Manly stuff.

MF: Why was the ethos so nationalist?

PB: I can understand why they were nationalist now. It's a good thing. There's nothing wrong with nationalism in its pure sense. It is the love of your native place, what's part of you. It was nice to be introduced to that. But that was never going to be the cornerstone of my self-image. I was always looking outwards, outside of my locality, and I was never going to get locked into the sense that locality is the most important thing in your consciousness.

I perceived it as very academically obsessive, and without much thought as to a broader consciousness. Maybe it's unfair to criticise that ethic (if it indeed that was the ethic) because those were hard times and Catholics were still on the way up, you know? Fighting hard.

MF: Did you feel yourself also to be part of Derry City while at St. Columb's?

PB: I never really integrated with Derry. The day-boys coming in the gate every day and going home to their mammies at night were a whole different breed. You almost didn't allow yourself to associate with them, because you'd start wondering about why you weren't going home to your mammy. Derry City to me was always a weird place, strange place. I've met lots of day-boys since, like Jimmy Sharkey. What they say about Derry indicates to me that it was a very oppressive place; that everybody was watching everybody else, and everybody was afraid somebody else would get a wee bit further than them. While people were trying to push themselves up, there was something else trying to push them down which was almost self-induced.

MF: What impact did the 1947 Education Act have on St. Columb's?

PB: St. Columb's is a great example of a school that benefited from the 1947 Education Act. That's what enabled the Catholic community in Northern Ireland to get ahead – education. Getting ahead was everything, and culture was probably a luxury.

MF: What is your harshest memory of St. Columb's?

PB: There was a period of three years perhaps where I was seriously bullied in St. Columb's by one person. That was something that I tried to talk about to my parents. They actually went to talk to the president about it on one occasion, but the vibe that came down from that meeting to me was that well, 'are you sure he isn't exaggerating a little bit?' And it was brushed over. I kind of felt, I've done all I can to stop this and it's not going to stop, so keep your head down again. But I was seriously bullied for three years, or it could have been even four. I don't even want to mention the person's name. But I hope he's very unhappy. This person had a fascination with me. He liked music, and had a fascination with me because I was musically talented. And wanted me always to play for him, but there was always an implied threat there that if I didn't, he would hit me. It was like as if I was this fascinating creature that this person was drawn towards but also wanted to destroy.

MF: Can you describe what kind of violence it was?

PB: It was the threat of violence. I never allowed myself to do anything that would actually bring it into reality, but the threat of violence was there. It was a very violent relationship, very violent. That hugely coloured my time in St. Columb's, and I've never actually spoken about that before. The weird thing about it was that he actually liked the music I played, and got quite excited when I played, particularly if I played Jerry Lee Lewis on the piano or Little Richard. There was some kind of sickness there that wanted to crush me at the same time as experience me.

MF: Did anything positive emerge from such tough experiences?

PB: The old cliché, you know, it makes a man out of you: it's not that untrue because everything that I am now and every strength I have, I've forged within myself as a result of these experiences. Why I am still so much an outsider and seemingly intractable, according to some people, is because nobody is ever going to dominate me again.

MF: It was purgatorial?

PB: Purgatory is a good way of describing it. But I mean, what did I need to be purged of?

MF: What do you say to people who actually liked St. Columb's?

PB: I went recently to one of these reunions where Jimmy Sharkey was being inducted into the St. Columb's Hall of Fame. I couldn't get over how many people I met there who thought it was a great place. It's all down to the individual.

MF: What was Dublin like when you arrived there?

PB: Dublin again might have been Timbuktu to me. I'd never been to Dublin in my life. I'd never been to Belfast. We went down to Dublin and we applied to UCD and I got accepted, so I went to Dublin in October of '64. Dublin was huge, a great release. My parents knew nothing about Dublin. They had no associations with Dublin. They had nobody in Dublin who they could call and say, 'will you check out what Paul's up to?' I think what St. Columb's did was teach me how to be on my own.

MF: So you began to flourish in Dublin?

PB: I had refused to let that artistic sensibility in me develop, because I felt it wouldn't be appreciated. I subconsciously kept it down until I left the college. It was only when I came to Dublin and started to get the stirrings that I would maybe do this for a living. In the flat below was this fellow called Mick Moloney, and he played Irish folk music. Suddenly I developed a relationship with these boys in the flat down below, and I remember picking up the first Bob Dylan album and thinking it sounded shite. I got asked to join this group The Johnstons by Mick Moloney. They were huge in Ireland, and I got asked to join. I saw that quite venally as a way to jump, shortcut, into a successful professional musical set-up, without having to climb my way up.

MF: How would you assess the legacy of Bob Dylan?

PB: Bob Dylan: cultural icon of the twentieth century, undoubtedly. He opened the doors for literature to enter popular music, for popular music to deal with more adult themes rather than just adolescent themes.

He loves Irish music. Three of the songs that I brought to public consciousness, he also has recorded. He recorded 'Arthur McBride'. He recorded 'The Lakes of Pontchartrain'. Oh no, he maybe did that live. Most recently, 'Mary and the Soldier' is on his new album. I know where he heard those. He heard them on the album that I did with Andy Irvine, and my album after that.

MF: An aspect of this film is that all the participants are going back to St. Columb's after years away. How do you feel about returning for the first time since you left?

PB: It's interesting going back to the school. It'll be a totally different place. I'm actually fascinated. I've often wanted to go back to St. Columb's and walk up those stairs and go into the room that I slept in for four years, and see it once more. Maybe it's a little bit of closure I'm looking for in doing this film.

It'll be confusing for me, because I'll be mostly with day-boys. John Hume was my French teacher. Phil Coulter was a day-boy. He knows nothing about what I'm talking about. It is easy to have a rose-tinted view of St. Columb's if you were a day-boy.

A Conversation with Seamus Deane and Seamus Heaney, Moderated by Maurice Fitzpatrick

In November 1985, Fintan O'Toole edited a conversation between Heaney and Joseph Brodsky for *Magill*, after Heaney hit the streets in protest against the hanging of Benjamin Moloise in South Africa. A similar on camera conversation seemed ideal for St. Columb's. A conversation between Seamus Deane and Seamus Heaney took place on the last day of principal photography. We filmed it in the old museum of St. Columb's where prefects used to 'bash' young boarders. The other participants had been filmed *en groupe* over the weekend and had returned home. It was now Tuesday and it was Heaney and Deane. Sharkey quipped that the King and Queen had arrived and the regency had to make way for them.

Whatever about their regality, the two have had, in several ways, parallel life trajectories. Deane says, interestingly, about his educational formation, 'We went in there raw and came out cooked'. St. Columb's can be seen as an institution that took the tabula rasa and made the impression. I suggested in pre-interview that this conversation would dwell on what they had in common. 'It should be over soon then,' was Deane's response. In an essay about his classmate and university mate, 'The Famous Seamus', Deane wrote about their friendship up to the moment of the Nobel Prize ceremony; the fact that they are namesakes; that they came through school and university together; that they have found in each other's backgrounds something to stimulate each other's creative natures. Their paths interwove in many ways throughout their lives and it seemed to have a spectral connection to the fact that they are namesakes. The myth of the day-boy and boarder distinction was mutually created, and later latched upon by critics, as Deane explains.

The problem of Seamus the day-boy and Seamus the boarder seemed to finally find a moment of clarity on the eve of our filming them together. We had used the old museum of St. Columb's a lot already and many of the lighting possibilities had been explored. The cameraman, the director and several others of the crew were sitting at the dinner table trying to find a way to frame them without repeating ourselves. Suddenly, someone sketched two stick men with a speech bubble coming from one of their mouths, which read, 'Hi, I'm Seamus'.

In *The Listener*, on 24 October 1968, Heaney wrote about the civil rights march which had been baton-charged in Derry on October 5th. Today everyone refers to that moment simply as the beginning of the Troubles. On October 5th, the unionist state felt affronted and were miffed as a result. The human, if pig-headed, response is, 'I'll go down rather than submit to these guys'. Heaney was not present in the city – he held a lecturing position in Queen's University, Belfast. But, in the essay he wrote for *The Listener* a fortnight later, he tells the story of his return to the city where he received his grammar school education. It is a journey in many senses. He reviews the way things were and the way things were destined to change as a result of the civil rights campaign. If the tone of the piece seems nationalist, it must be noted that Heaney's statements have a factual basis.

'As I drove into Derry, two buildings dominated the hill ahead. One was the solid grey bulk of the gaol; the other, the many-windowed front of the school where I had spent six years as a boarder. In those six years, we were rarely allowed into the town and spent much of our leisure time on a treadmill of walks insides the college walls ... [we used to] chant about the only human rights we were interested in then:

"This time four weeks, where shall we be?
Outside the gates of slaveree!"

Now, ten years later, the gaol has been closed but walls and walks still remain powerful symbols in the Derry imagination.'

The charge of 'wrecking the new moderation' was levelled at Catholics (the civil rights movement was predominantly, though not exclusively, Catholic in its make-up) who marched at this time. Gradual shifts in Northern Ireland were undoubtedly happening, but for underprivileged Catholics those shifts were unacceptably gradual given the circumstances of their lives. Given the conditions in which Catholics lived, the civil rights movement was inevitable. If unionists look back and honestly ask themselves, 'what if we had have granted those rights?', the Troubles could have been avoided. The IRA gave unionists an excuse not to examine the situation rigorously. The charge against Derry Catholics of wrecking the peace, it must be remembered, came most vociferously from Conor Cruise O'Brien, living in suburban Dublin. By suggesting that 'we would be better off without the trouble-maker from Thebes' – a code word for the character Antigone who to him represented the civil rights movement – O'Brien aligns himself with the Orange State and those who upheld it. His use of the Antigone analogy, as means of showing the complexity of political protest in a highly volatile situation, is a means of concealing that agenda. O'Brien's argument is that state violence must be respected; and that even in a situation where state violence is deeply corrupt, to disrespect the state's monopoly on violence is to irresponsibly imperil people: 'Peace depends upon the acceptance of civil subordination since the powerful will use force to uphold their laws.' If the threat that Antigone embodies were done away with, very little would be lost, but it is true 'that this way of imagining and dramatising man's dignity maybe expresses the essence of what man's dignity actually is. In losing it, man might gain peace at the price of his soul' (*The Listener*, 24 October 1968). This edition of *The Listener* awakened the 29-year-old Heaney to the vast political implications of the play, *Antigone*. He was later to write a version of the play in 2004. The complexity of the debate initiated by October 5th was, Deane argues, 'vulgarised by O'Brien among others'.

Similarly, on the question of the ratification of state violence, O'Brien's will to preserve the old order and reconstruct it from within conflicts with Deane's condemnation of a system that he had seen to be irredeemably corrupt.

What insulates Northern Catholic history writers from the revisionist perspective is the memory of the state that they were faced with as children. This knowledge of the colonial context remains. McCann, who is no nationalist by his own admission, wrote cogently about the machinations of the state which northern Catholics faced if they called a strike or protest.

Heaney wrote at this time that if Catholics were to retain self-respect, they must seek justice for the wrongs of October 5th – which inevitably meant provoking the security forces of the state. O'Brien's premise was that nationalists would have to undergo the violence they provoked. Deane, in this interview, exposes the hypocrisy of a state that 'will always be given the excuse that it is the state'. Again, three panels on the triptych of political response to October 5th are evident. That October 5th was a huge event is borne out by the complexity of the response it elicited. Heaney assesses Conor Cruise O'Brien with reservations about his consistency. Deane is more condemnatory.

The October 5th protest incurred the full ire of the riot police. As Heaney put it, 'television *revealed* the zeal of the police' [Italics mine]. Here Heaney's terminology echoes Deane's. It seemed to Heaney and many others that October 5th would cause many people in the North to crawl out from behind their protective armour: the political positions of generations were entirely undermined. This march caused many who had never believed in political action to become politicised, to debate the foundations of the unjust society in which they lived. An ancillary effect of October 5th was its centring the scandal of the Northern Irish state in Derry. With its majority Catholic population, Derry civil rights advocates would always be able to marshal support that would over-

whelm the local police. So the situation was immediately pushed to its logical conclusion – an affront to the very existence of the state – and it was dealt with as such. Writing about the same event, Deane credited McCann as being one of the organisers who gave the march its socialist thrust; and the march itself as that which 'began the revelation to the Bogside' ('Why Bogside', *The Honest Ulsterman*, 1971).

Heaney's insight that Catholics had, after the assault, to agitate more stridently was quite accurate. He anticipated that the opposition of liberalism on the nationalist side by the unyielding unionist agenda had the potential to escalate into much worse conflict. The hope of 'small rapprochements and readjustments were being made. Minimal shifts in different areas – artistic, educational, political – were beginning to effect new contacts and concessions' (*Finders Keepers*, p. 46) was to prove in vain.

Recalcitrant unionists hark back to this moment – October 5th – and identify it as the time when a sufficient number of people handed the reins to potentially violent groups. When nationalists hark back, they see it as the moment when unionism failed to exhibit enough decency and that failure enabled violent groups to engage in terrorism.

Deane speaks of those same presuppositions limiting artistic work – and the need to get beyond them. It is key that his disenchantment (and the disenchantment of other Northern writers) with the foundation of the state caused this need to transcend the Northern situation as it was constituted.

One of the consequences of the civil rights movement and the subsequent Troubles, was that society looked to writers – with some justification – to somehow interpret events on the street in their art. Heaney has often seemed a reluctant commentator on the political situation in the North, entering the debate more out of a sense of duty than volition. When his name was included in an anthology of British poets, he joked that he would have to correct that to stay on good terms with his wife. The central rebuff, however, is unequivocal. The Field Day publishing phenomenon was the appropriate organ for his response.

> 'A British one, is characterized
> As British. But don't be surprised
> If I demur for, be advised
> My passport's green.
> No glass of ours was ever raised
> To toast The Queen.'
> ('An Open Letter', *Field Day Pamphlets*, 1983, Stanza No. 14).

Heaney has at times approached the Troubles of the North tentatively. He met Danny Morrison on the train going north, and he did not acquiesce with the Sinn Féin man's will to write 'something for us'. Morrison, who had coined the phrase 'with an armalite in one hand and a ballot box in the other', was rebuked by Heaney, who said that when he writes, he writes for himself. Deane has written more directly about the Troubles and he mentions his essay, 'The Writer and the Troubles' (1974), in this interview. Deane's own writings have always been characterised by a very definite political position and concern. In the interview quoted below, Deane suggested that Heaney and others should adopt a more overtly political stance.

SD: Do you think that if some political stance is not adopted by you and the Northern poets at large, this refusal might lead to a dangerous strengthening of earlier notions of the autonomy of poetry and corroborate the recent English notion of the happy limitations of a 'well made poem?' And furthermore, do you feel that this disdain of poetry for all that would break its own autonomy could lead to the sponsoring of a literature which would be almost deliberately minor?

SH: I think it could ...

SD: Do you think it has?

SH: Most poetry is inevitably so ...

SD: But not deliberately so!'

('Unhappy and at Home: Interview with Seamus Heaney' by Seamus Deane, *Crane Bag*, 1977)

An example of a writer taking a self-consciously political stance comes in the following riposte. Deane takes Conor Cruise O'Brien to task for seeking to attribute the cause of the Troubles to the Catholic side.

'I think it should be pointed out to your readers that Conor Cruise O'Brien, in reviewing Jimmy Breslin's *World Without End, Amen* [21 February 1974] contrives to give a version of the situation which is quite as distorted as he claims Breslin's to be. He is, after all, the minister of Propaganda in the Republic, exercising a severe censorship through radio and television, and a slightly more subtle one through the Government Information Bureau, which he reconstructed by drafting into it men who would faithfully reproduce his own views of events in the North.

He makes the implication that the Provisional IRA began the killing in the North. Not so. It was the Royal Ulster Constabulary who did this, using armoured cars and Browning machine guns on unarmed and unsuspecting Catholic citizens in the Falls Road area in 1969. He also states that the British army's role in the North is, fundamentally, to protect the Catholic population. This was originally so, but to state that this situation persists is a lie. Who protects the Catholics from the massive campaign of Protestant assassination gangs (accounting now for over 220 deaths of the 1,000 O'Brien snidely attributes to the IRA)? The British army has killed scores of innocent Catholics in various areas – Bogside, New Lodge Road, Strahane, Bally-murphy, and many other places. That army has killed a further 80 civilians in what are euphemistically called road accidents since it came to Northern Ireland four years ago. These deaths are the consequence, in most cases, of a campaign against the Catholic populations of the main Catholic ghettos in Belfast and Derry, one favorite form of which is the high-speed driving of armoured cars through heavily populated areas, day and night, but often without lights and often with two wheels on the footpath.

I have seen many examples of this, one fatal, in Derry, my home town. There is also considerable evidence that the notorious British army SAS units are operating in the North, bombing and assassinating, chiefly, although not exclusively, in Catholic areas ...' (*The New York Review of Books*, 30 May 1974).

O'Brien responded to this by saying it would require a lot of cool-headedness to make the Sunningdale Agreement work.

'Some academics, on both sides of the fence, have contributed to the rising level of verbal violence, thereby increasing the momentum towards Civil War. Mr. Deane's letter is an average specimen of this kind.'

O'Brien's language is vaguely threatening. Given that O'Brien exercised censorship in his capacity as a minister, his roles as a writer and as a politician blur here: censure spilling into the threat of censorship. O'Brien implies that he is almost uniquely able to spot inflammatory language; and that politics have come to such a pass in the North that any writer who uses 'verbal violence' is liable to be punished for it. What O'Brien is less quick to address is how British special intelligence agents had penetrated the Irish government, as Deane argued, and how this infiltration compromised some of Ireland's government ministers who were in no position to be trusted. On 1 October 1971, the Minister for Posts and Telegraphs invoked the Section 31 broadcasting ban to curb RTÉ from broadcasting exposure of illegal organisations such as the IRA. This was two months after the British army had introduced internment without trial. Such governmental restrictions gave rise to a self-censoring tendency that lasted through the next four decades.

It is unsurprising that when politics become so constraining people looked to art to give an extra dimension to an understanding of the political situation. As Deane argued in his individual interview, the separation of art and politics – in St. Columb's and elsewhere in colonised societies – was a political position that was at pains to pretend it was not one. O'Brien's reading of *Antigone* froze Northern Irish politics and classical art in one frame. It is hard to overestimate the influence O'Brien's reading of *Antigone* exerted. It became possible for Deane, say, whose aversion to O'Brien's line is obvious, to engage on the same subject even if he ultimately argues against it. Like an asymptote in reverse, Deane and O'Brien start at almost the same point but forever pull away towards conclusions that can never be reconciled with each other. This was a point in Northern Irish history when radical social change induced major internal change in people. It became natural for some Catholics to discredit Remembrance Sunday celebrations which they had once taken part in; for others, that burying of a part of Catholic heritage was wrong and could only damage its practitioners. Heaney once commented about standing for God Save the Queen:

> 'You're caught between the courtesies of upwardly mobile middle-class culture and the drag into the nationalist solidarities. So there was a kind of a stooping policy ... standing and not standing. It's still not quite resolved.' (Interview with Vincent Browne, *The Irish Times*)

This dual interview also explores the Field Day dramatic and publishing achievement. Field Day was a collegiate enterprise. Half of Field Days' directors (Friel, Heaney and Deane) were St. Columb's Boys. Deane speaks of maieutic knowledge, which here means an approach, often through questioning or novel demonstration of something already known, to help an audience discover their own connection to it.

For example, Deane likened the public awe at the hunger strikers to a public drama being played out in Northern Irish society at large. Field Day's directors – Seamus Heaney, Seamus Deane, Brian Friel, Stephen Rea, David Hammond and Tom Paulin – managed to generate through their theatrical and literary efforts much valuable debate in Ireland. Seamus Heaney's comment that Seamus Deane has given us exhilaration in all his work could equally be applied to Heaney's own work: when history is written it will record that the Seamuses have done the state some service.

MF: [to SH] What were the circumstances in which you found yourself when you wrote for *The Listener* in the late 1960s?

SH: The sense of answerability to what was going on was present in all kinds of ways from the start. It was felt by anybody from our generation coming up, being published, and being seen to have a voice or heard to have a voice as part of the Northern minority. And that became even more pronounced after October 5th, 1968, I would say. In fact that was the first time that I wrote about Derry. Earlier, I was allowed access to the *New Statesman* by Karl Miller. I did a piece for a series that was called significantly 'Out of London' – because those were the days when London was the centre entirely. Paisley was on the go at that time, some time about 1965/66. Then Miller moved to *The Listener*. I would date the sense of being representative from the moment I did 'Old Derry's

Walls' in *The Listener* a week or two after the 5th of October 1968
– after the baton-charging of the civil rights march here. That made the
sense of answerability more explicit and more pointed. Ever after that
there was some sense of that overarching representativeness.

MF: [to SH] In that historic edition of *The Listener*, Conor Cruise
O'Brien wrote an essay that seems to have had a major effect on your
outlook. He wrote that non-violent protest elicits violence, using the
example of Sophocles' *Antigone*. Can you describe the circumstances of
that issue of *The Listener*?

SH: Miller had commissioned the piece from Conor Cruise O'Brien.
O'Brien had actually spoken – I'd attended a meeting in Queen's University – just a week or so before this march: he had spoken of civil disobedience as a tactic to contest unjust situations. He had talked about
Gandhi, of course. One of the things he said was if you do this, you
have to be prepared to undergo the violence that you provoke. In *The
Listener* article he took up the analogy of *Antigone*, the play and the
character, who basically insists on rights which are against the law of
the state. Her sense of right is not the state's sense of what is lawful. She
is a moral and spiritual hero, but she brings down violence upon herself and violence upon those around her. And Cruise O'Brien used her
thrillingly as a figure of nobility and ambiguity at that point. In a sense,
he gave street protest high cultural ratification, provided an imaginative
dimension for political action. Something which he would renege on, of
course. Eventually he would change his attitude entirely.

MF [to SD]: This all relates to the theme of the responsibility of the artist in a time of unrest. Yeats once agonised, 'Did that play of mine send
out/Certain men the English shot?' (*The Man and the Echo*). How do
you see the role of the artist in conflict situations?

SD: I don't know how I could assess such a thing. I'm uncomfortable
with the very idea that there is such an agency, such an entity that is
in some way measurable. When you say responsibility, it's responsibility for what? For the articulation of a dilemma? Or responsibility for
bringing it on? Or responsibility for showing the complications of it?
Responsibility for finding some humane ground in the light of which

all political positions are going to look either fundamentally similar or like simply different sections of one fan? I think the danger always with the writer and the Troubles (I remember I wrote an essay with that title somewhere around then [1974]) is that you're going to say what makes the arts, and most especially in this country the literary arts, different from politics is that they offer a humane ground which is more capacious and more hospitable to all sorts of political positions than, for instance, the support of any one political position itself. And I have serious reservations about that particular pose – to find this humane ground – on the part of the arts. But it's one of the poses that the arts have had for a couple of hundred years, in the light of which all political positions can always be made to look doctrinaire or narrow or in some way partial, partisan.

At the same time, there is a capacity in a work of art for velleities of sympathy, which are not possible within the realm of political action. But in relation, for instance, to what you were speaking of, the use of *Antigone*, it seems to me that when you pose the question, over here, in the left hand corner, there's ancestral piety; and over here, in the right hand corner, there is unflinching political will. And the battle is to be joined between them, and the battle is always tragic. Well, in a sense, once the prescription is written in those terms, the sympathies are prescribed and redistributed straight away. The state will always be given the excuse that it is the state, after all, and therefore it will be provoked to violence for which those who provoke it must feel responsible rather than the state itself be revealed to have been pandemically violent in all of its actions. Especially a state like the state we were faced with, that says that it decries violence, whereas in fact it's founded on it. And I think that sort of in and out debate which began with some promise, as Seamus was saying, in those early years, was very quickly vulgarised (by O'Brien among others) into a kind of partisan political position, the ultimate result of which was the ratification of state violence. And ancestral pieties were then somehow mutated into some kind of retrograde or regressive tribal chanting, Orphic chanting, that went on in the background. The idea of it being a tragic collision is repeated time and again in history, as if it is something that belongs to the human condition. It's very difficult to engage in that debate without almost immediately becoming bound up with what looks like an analysis, but is in fact a set of presuppositions.

MF: [to SH] When Field Day was founded, political concerns were very much to the fore. How did Field Day come about?

SH: Well, it grew from the production of the play *Translations* [1980] by Brian Friel and Stephen Rea. It seemed at that moment to all their friends, some of whom were my friends, that something had been stirred in the whole country, that theatre was activating and allowing questions to come to the fore again, wakening up the whole society. My recollection is that all of us were saying to Brian and Stephen, you mustn't let this go, you must do something else. The result was that shortly afterwards, we were asked to come to a meeting in the Gresham Hotel. Seamus, myself, David Hammond, Tom Paulin were along with the other two. My recollection is that at that meeting Seamus sketched out the idea of a re-reading of Irish literature, an up-to-date anthology. The idea of doing pamphlets was also mooted and the hope was that the poets (Seamus, Tom Paulin and myself) might get involved in theatre. David Hammond was there also as a kind of imaginative energy, a straddler of two traditions, as it were. So there was an idea that we might change the game and get past these heraldic pro and con positions that are all over the North and South of the country. Actually, we were lucky to have Seamus' intellectual vigour and articulation of our aims. He in a sense wrote our mission statement. He was an invigorating, exciting presence for us. He wrote two of the pamphlets [*Civilians and Barbarians*, 1983; *Heroic Styles: The Tradition of an Idea*, 1984] which were epoch-making, I think.

SD: Looking back on it now, and trying to remember with some precision what happened in the early days, it seems to me that one of the things that we were attempting to do was to create – I'm going to use the phrase 'create an audience', because it's a well-worn phrase from Yeats – but it wasn't so much create an audience that hadn't been there. This was to make visible or bring out an audience that already was there. Partly because of what had happened in the North, it was on the point of articulating a sense of itself, which everyone felt was in some sense in the offing, in the atmosphere, but which we felt, especially via theatre, could be dramatised and displayed. The theatre was wonderfully successful in achieving that, in creating a discourse that people would recognise almost instantly and felt that they in many ways had already possessed. What we used to call maieutic knowledge, where you find words for something and only when you hear those words you realise you already knew it. That was one of the magical effects of the theatre, for me. I mean pretty consistently, through all the theatrical productions, and through the whole experiment, that was one of the pervasive charms of it. Not that we were breaking into new territory, but that we were discovering that new territory had already been broken into, but simply hadn't been sufficiently recognised.

SH: That was actually there in a way with Brian mocking his own achievements in *Translations* with the play *The Communication Cord*. The irony that everybody had within themselves even about their passionate beliefs was a very modern, even almost a post-modern ploy of Brian Friel's at that time. It knocked earnestness out of the thing a bit. So the ambiguities and the velleities, as Seamus said, were implicit in the make-up of the board and in the different plays, plays about English/Irish identity – *Saint Oscar* by Terry Eagleton, *Double Cross* by Tom Kilroy – about the relationship between the islands. It wasn't just a matter of 'Ulster is British' or 'Ulster is Uladh'. The total, complicated cultural and political nexus that we lived in was our subject.

SD: But you're always just skimming the waves. We felt that we were achieving a certain degree of complication and complexity, but we knew that there was just a gossamer thin divide and we would be back into the old bigotries and the fixed positions. You have to be flexible to avoid paralysis, but you knew that the flexibility was the more intensely sought because the paralysis was always so close, and in a flash you could be seized by it.

MF: Field Day caused a lot of consternation. Could you speak a little about that?

SH: Well, its aims were constantly being discovered, and its action was constantly being reinvented. I do think that the record stands and stands admirably, not to say nobly. There were all the plays that were put on. There were the pamphlets that were put out. There was the *Anthology of Irish Writing* that Seamus edited as General Editor, a mighty achievement. Controversially received, it stirred up action, but it is there as a *monumentum*. People who assailed it actually use it now in teaching. It went on, of course, to breed a further two volumes. More important – when history comes to be written – the activities, the debates, the provocations, all were part of the age and the time. I think both in terms of publication, in terms of dramatic performance, in terms of the agitation, stimulation, consolidation of a different people's imaginative, artistic and general psychic social life, it was a good thing for us all to be there together. It helped individually. It gave sense and meaning to individual enterprises, which would have been proceeding anyway, but there was a sense of community endeavour. I think each (and I don't think this is to exaggerate) individual got different things from it. But there were benefits for the audience too, obviously.

SD: I would generally agree with that. My feeling is that with any such enterprise, if it has any success, it begins to be absorbed into the system as we call it. Then it seems to somehow have become respectable, become part of the landscape. There's a short parable by Franz Kafka on

that, where he speaks about the priests who used to look after the sacred temple and all its precious objects. One night panthers, great cats, broke into the temple and scattered the sacred ornaments and generally created mayhem. And despite increasing security, night by night, this continued to happen until finally the priests decided to make the panther break-ins part of the ritual. That very often happens in any sort of movement that begins by saying we want to in some way modify or upset or even violate those things that are supposed to be sacred and inviolable. And then it suddenly finds itself having become respectable, and then one suddenly feels something wrong here, you know, because you have been absorbed. So there's a degree of absorption, but there is always. I think since Field Day, in a publishing sense, still survives, there's always the sense that the initial impetus from those early years, especially from the 1980s, that there was always some way to turn this out again, to whet the knife-edge and to keep probing, even as one is being absorbed into a landscape, political or social or literary, whatever it may be, which is nevertheless not the landscape with which one began. So there is an absorption and an experimentation going on simultaneously.

MF: [to SH] I'd like to ask you about your friendship. It started here in St. Columb's and grew beyond that ...

SH: Well, the school friendship was the start of it – we were parallel in class from our first year in St. Columb's to the last year. But in our final year the two of us were in a group of four. A kind of bonding occurred then. We went to Queen's in a group, it has to be said, with a sense of Derry identity, boarders and day-boys together. Then Seamus and I ended up in the English department as students, Honours English students. So that was a very amicable and energetic group. We retained a kind of St. Columb's College glee and private language, a mocking fondness. Then, after Queen's, Seamus went off to Derry and on to Cambridge. We met again after I came down to Dublin in 1972, when Seamus was teaching in UCD. We had both separately grown up. But not necessarily grown separate. There was a kind of new energy, and again, a new connection – a much more serious and intellectually stimulating, and imaginatively helpful engagement for me at that point. So from there on into Field Day. I would say it was from the beginning a rich and rare relationship.

SD: My sense of it is that there was always at the heart of it this perennial and (certainly to outsiders) monotonous joke about the day-boy/boarder contrast. Yet I sort of enjoyed the ways in which that could be manipulated, not with great ingenuity, the way in which it could be used as a sort of instrument of distinction and difference, while at the same time still being commonly held. I was reading in Seamus' just published book of interviews with Dennis O'Driscoll: that is mentioned again. O'Driscoll had asked him did he think that I was more given to abstract thought as opposed to the kind of rumination one associates with poetry. My reaction is first to say the distinction itself is fake from the outset. And then I thought, oh, here we go, we can use this for the boarder/day-boy again (I said boarder/day-boy). Conceptual thought, abstract thought and poetic sensuousness – let's say the realisation of the concrete universal in a poem, and the abstraction from it in a concept – suddenly have become now, in a ghostly way, characteristic features of the way we both behave as writers. In one way, I want to say it's junk. In another sense, I want to say it's wonderful how this little instrument can actually keep opening these questions that are recurrent because one is always trying to find a way out of the banality of the question. It's very difficult to say something is really banal if it is endlessly fertile. I think that that's a strange thing: fertility and banality are first cousins.

MF: [to SH] One important moment in the path of your time together seems to have been a trip to the Gaeltacht. What do you remember of that time?

SH: Well, it was during our time at Queen's. To tell you the truth, it is a luminous memory for me but it isn't there in very much detail. I myself wasn't studying Irish at Queen's, nor indeed was Seamus. But our friends were studying it. It was at Easter time. It was a break away from Belfast. It was a break away from the usual. It was good weather up on the Atlantic Drive. We had the company of women that we were fond of – it was idyllic. It was just an otherwhere, a holiday. No great revelations or changes occurred; but it was what Wordsworth would call a 'spot of time'. In my memory, it has a lovely shine off it. The landscape of Donegal, the sea, the air, all that lift that occurs when you're across the border of the usual, into the elsewhere.

SD: And still it bespeaks to me of youth. Energy, light and youth. We all know how much nonsense is talked about tradition and how much tradition is invented and so forth, but seeing the Gaeltacht then at that time was actually a revelation of something really existent that was different from anything that I had known. It was the first time I actually went anywhere where I felt within this place there is still what used to be called a utopian possibility. If you could have a kind of a social or political life that included this, wasn't entirely made up of it, but included this kind of possibility and magic, then that would permit you to believe in emancipation or utopia without being foolish, because you'd actually seen the momentary appearance of it, in those days in Donegal.

SH: Also, I think for myself, as one of the boarders in the mix, we were all a bit older – we weren't at St. Columb's any more. We had glimpsed some possibility of a free and new life for ourselves individually. There was Dicky McGown, I remember, and Seamus Bonner, guys who were senior to us in St. Columb's. There was a comitatus. There was a sense of the boys of St. Columb's as well as the girls of the district changing into young, possible individuals. I think that was also in the air somehow. You felt that you had gone ahead a wee bit, and you were on your own a wee bit more, and you were together also as a group.

SD: Yeah, I think we went in there raw and came out cooked in some ways.

MF: [to SH] I read somewhere – I do not know how much credibility to give this – that in Queen's Seamus Deane was known as a poet of great promise, whereas Seamus Heaney was a dab hand at essay-writing.

SH: Well, Seamus Deane was the poet that put the wind up all of us in Queen's University. He had a sort of high style and, as I have said elsewhere, a definite sense of calling. He had that more than any of us, and retained it in different ways all through until now. We were dependent upon him for poetic energy and for insight, and example. I would say also in terms of the lifelong friendship of writerly enterprise, another St. Columb's person who was central to us both was the playwright Brian Friel. Brian was not in any way a mentor, but I think he kept his eye on us. He was very dear to us as a third person, a third party. I feel that our friendship was sustained among other things by having Friel as a senior friend, an invigilator of sorts, who was a playwright of world stature as well as your pal.

SD: I mean, I'd agree with that. In some ways of course it's invidious to be putting oneself in relation to Seamus' spectacular career as a writer. But I would think if one thinks of friendship and form, so to speak, I think of Seamus in relation to poetry, I think of Friel in relation to plays, obviously, and myself I think of in relation to essays, the essay as a form. But in a way the essay as an art form. I don't mean the sort of sherry and biscuits essay of the common room type. I mean the kind of essay I'd associate with say someone like Walter Benjamin. And it took me a long time to realise that in fact the pursuit of that form is something that's very elusive. But I learned something about being able to write in the essay form by trying to write about Seamus' poetry, by trying to write about Brian Friel's theatre, by trying to write those things for Field Day, where in a sense it's not just a matter of being analytic or polemical. It's a way of combining those energies in such a way that they're only component parts of a kind of meditation.

SH: And exhilaration. Hugh McDiarmuid's definition of poetry applies to essays. McDiarmuid says poetry is 'human existence come to life'. I think that's what Seamus has achieved as well, in verse, through prose, through everything he's done. It's a brilliant remark, isn't it? 'Human existence come to life'.

Conclusion

On October 9th, 2008, Heaney attended the operatic premiere of his version of *Antigone, The Burial at Thebes*, in the Globe Theatre, London. On October 5th the fortieth anniversary of the historic civil rights march took place in Derry, commemorating a march which Eamonn McCann had helped to start all those years ago. What do these events have in common? Forty years on, the same debate pulses in the minds of these writers. When McCann says that he regrets that he did not see the ferocity of nationalism coming (beneath the mask of a socialist agenda) he is in dialogue with his younger self, a debate filtered through four decades of experience. When Heaney suggests that the characters Antigone and her sister Ismene represent two opposing parts of our being, he is perhaps also talking about the young and the older Heaney. When he quotes Conor Cruise O'Brien's views on *Antigone* and says that they portray 'the twists and turns of Cruise O'Brien's views in years to come', Heaney is also suggesting that he himself has negotiated those same mental contours. His own re-reading of *Antigone* began with the student-led march, organised under a socialist banner by McCann. His re-reading of the play has evidently gone on all his life.

The intriguing aspect of *Antigone* is that nobody who reads it properly ever gets to answer the question: at what point does non-violent protest become legitimate? And to allow that non-violent protest is legitimate, how to account for the cumulative consequences that flow from it? This dilemma came down even to personal choices. If they did not go to Belfast, the university-educated in Ulster were disposed to go to Dublin rather than London. Because of Orange discrimination, they looked outside the six counties. At the same time, Northerners realised that the Republic was poorer. Northerners were conscious of the role of the British subsidy in the burgeoning Northern economy in the 1950s. This doublethink was part of their background from the start. They have seen the problem through the prism of a lot of pain, a lot that had been preventable. As McCann put it:

> 'People's view of the '60s reflects their interests and needs. Those who have given up on revolution need to rubbish revolutionary ideas. One reason that certain of the '60s generation now propound a view of the period in line with what the ruling class said then is that they, themselves, have become agents of the ruling class in the interim... The fact that things worked out the way they did doesn't mean they couldn't have worked out differently.' (*War and Peace in Northern Ireland*, p. 3)

The Eleven Plus was the lifeline for this generation. Families did not look askance at it. Families, particularly those from Derry City, had a distinct feeling from the outset that 1947 would break the unionist hold. That feeling was there and found articulation in the first civil rights march on October 5th, 1968, which, in Deane's words, 'began the revelation to the Bogside'. October 5th catapulted many people into the civil rights movement, partly because it was the logical conclusion of the expectation that had been put on their shoulders since their entry into grammar school. They had emerged, 'bright and unmannerly as crowbars', as Heaney put it. They found a compass in education. Their identity evolved as they moved forward in education. Many from Derry City, much more than their rural counterparts, maintain that it did not take great prescience to see the consequences that 1947 would have. Apart from politics, some participants maintained that they would have done exactly what they did in their lives had they not gone to St. Columb's. Others claim that 'going to the college was the making of me'. McCann is slower to acknowledge St. Columb's postive aspects. Still, McCann's lauding the study of ancient languages and history as a means to gain a stronger perspective on our own world is arguably the biggest legacy of his education at St. Columb's. The understanding we gain of our own world when we learn about past civilisations was a perspective engendered by the St. Columb's education.

To reconcile a comment like 'the teachers were a decent cross-section of humanity' with a comment arguing that they 'should have been in prison for violence' is difficult. It is even harder given that both men whom I quote above were part not only of the same school but the same class in school. A writer has a duty to be fair to people's reputations, but a duty also to tell the truth.

This book is inevitably an examination of memory processes as well as the effect that 1947 had on St. Columb's. It is a cliché to say that the sun sets on vistas of our past. Not so in the case of the boys of St. Columb's. If pushed, I'd estimate that seventy per cent of the accounts I heard from students of this generation about their schooling were overall negative. Even the positive accounts have taints of negativity. Heaney, for example, records that 'the strap went epileptic on my first day ... [But I] still wrote home that things were not so bad ...' The optimistic habit of mind Heaney formed vis-à-vis St. Columb's endures to this day. Others, who decided against the place from the first day, reach to their respective vilifications.

One man I met wondered if the time really was repressed. A lot of the constraints were over their heads. To see this in a another way, young people from communist countries, say, who entered university after 1989 were hardly affected by the regime they had grown up with – they had the right to chose their own destinies. In Friel's play, *Molly Sweeney*, in the process of curing the protagonist, a doctor destroys her life. Maybe that is what happened in the North? Within the confines of an authoritarian state, they adapted. They were all harried and repressed, but hardly a day went past without his having moments of great happiness – often that came through solidarity. People can adapt if they have the nature to adapt. People today look on Northern Irish Catholics of this generation as having been ground down; and they were. But having grown up with it, many grew into it. They may have chafed at it a bit, but it did not reduce the laughter. It may have even increased it. While it is true that when being kept below a grinding poverty line it is hard to laugh, still, Daly remembers the Bogside as an area full of humour.

This book has been an attempt to show how the outcome of 1947 manifested itself. The causes of the transformation of the Catholic minority in the North was the result of a complex of forces – but education was the main dynamic because it gave form and articulation to the Catholic populace. In their several ways they go down in history as a very peaceful and civilised group of Catholics, undoing the unionist domination in the North. After they learned to survive in the unionist state, they then learned to thrive. The considerable momentum that gathered from their endeavour paved the way for future generations. Their achievement is still being felt today.

Hume said, 'when the history of St. Columb's is written the introduction of the Eleven Plus ...' and Coulter says – about John Hume and Austin Currie – 'when the history of that period comes to be written'. Similarly, Heaney says, speaking about the cause of consternation over Field Day, 'when history comes to be written ...' This book has compiled some of their history: I gathered the testimonies of those who were both products and, later, agents of that history. They 'broke some silences', as Heaney put it, and opened avenues that had been unimaginable to their parents.

On Coulter being offered Visiting Professor at Boston College, Heaney encouraged him to go and do it – without any sense of inferiority. The discipline in the semi-monastic institution taught the boys to be at ease with work: to take on work rather than try to get out of it. And through this work any residual inferiority complex modified to the point of extinction. What St. Columb's boys all have in common is that they all took initiatives – they liberated themselves through work because it was work that they chose. An outsider observing a group of St. Columb's boys in Queen's during the 1950s remarked, 'there is one thing for sure, St. Columb's boys are trained to work'.

Having gone through a crucible of discipline, they knew what it was to work hard. And it was admirable work: the great contribution of the boys of St. Columb's in the North was that they helped to reconstruct the Catholic identity. Learning to be free was not merely an individualistic venture. They faced the authority of Northern Ireland in a way that could not be ignored. They helped to establish equality in Northern Ireland through education. This book has been a history of that identity, an attempt to set forth the conflicts that their young selves faced and how their older selves reflect on them to show a key transformation in Ireland's history. What success the book has is attributable to the depth and fascination of such conflicts much more than how I set them forth. They were the generation that nearly caused the Education Act to be wrecked upon the rocks of religious controversy; they listened to stories about how 1947 would be the 'seeds of the fall of Stormont'; they discussed the political and emancipatory impact of their education while still at school; when they came of age they founded the civil rights movement. *Ní beidh a leithead ann arís.*

Appendix

Visual Script: The Boys of St. Columb's Treatment

The second part of this script is tentative. Filming inevitably departed considerably from this projection. Rather than reproduce here the actuality of filming, this treatment is printed because it formed the basis of our discussion of how to make the film and it is close to what the treatment looked like to begin with. – M.F.

As Europe was going to war and Ireland was isolated by its neutrality, a generation was born in Derry. It was to become the first generation of Catholics to receive free secondary education in the chequered history of the Northern Irish state. Born into poverty and a gerrymandered voting system that practically divested their community of property ownership, the boys who went to St. Columb's received a church Latin education under the British school system. The Irish language, too, was permitted. It was in this space of ecclesiastic thinking, Celticism and imperialism that the first group of educated Catholics found themselves. They were to become hugely influential, both in Ireland and abroad. Their voices have become synonymous with success in their chosen fields of music, politics, diplomacy and literature.

Set against the backdrop of today's political situation, oscillating between reconciliation and the continuing presence of tribal scars, the stories of these boys – men looking back on their boyhoods – will reconstruct the schooldays they had. It will focus mainly on the milieu out of which they grew rather than their successes in adult life. It will highlight how the hunger in their background imbued them with a will to realise their potential.

Heaney, Daly and Brady are the voices of outsiders who came to St. Columb's as boarders from the city's hinterland of County Derry, County Tyrone and County Fermanagh. They play an essential role in the narrative of the school which had been predominantly a boarding school. Excerpts from Seamus Heaney's first book of prose, *Preoccupations*, in particular his essay, 'From Mossbawn to Belfast', epitomise the condition of an outsider going to school in the city.

Deane, Sharkey and McCann are the voices of the ghetto, as it was then. Phil Coulter and John Hume came from areas nearby. They grabbed an education as it was the only way to lift themselves and, by extension, their community, out of the mire of a deeply corrupt political system. The boys were, several of them, close friends. In a way that they did not fully realise then, they were also allies due to the conditions under which they lived. Together they treaded the dangerous lines of official policing and governance that diverted the ends of power to deeper oppression.

The focus is on the school and the city of Derry in the 1940s, 1950s and 1960s. Any supplementary material will be used only to highlight the circumstances of the school and the schoolboys during the said period.

The school building of St. Columb's is still in use as a secondary school. Footage of the schoolboys of today will be used as a counterpoint to the post-war years. Images of the renovated Bogside will be used, as will pictures of Queen's University and other regional colleges. Photography of the city in general will be required – to emphasise the divide between the two sides of the Foyle river.

Images for rostrum shots from school albums, football team photographs, personal photographs of the interviewees, photographs of personages of the day, such as the famous teacher Sean B. O' Kelly, will be used. Above all, old photographs of the Bogside and the streets on the way to school will be enlarged and used to contrast with today's Derry, as the men look back on their boyhoods.

Interviews will form an integral part of this documentary. The quality and intellectual range of our interviewees will be an eloquent compliment to the montage work done in the editing room.

The protagonists are:

1933 – Edward Daly (Belleek, St. Columb's)
1937 – John Hume (Derry, St. Columb's, Nobelist 1998)
1939 – Seamus Deane (Bogside, St. Columb's)
1940 – Seamus Heaney (Mossbawn, St. Columb's, Nobelist 1995)
1942 – Phil Coulter (Abercorn Road, St. Columb's)
1942 – Eamonn McCann (Bogside, St. Columb's)
1945 – James Sharkey (Bogside, St. Columb's)
1947 – Paul Brady (Strabane, St. Columb's)

Everyone has confirmed that they will participate. Moreover, we have secured a helicopter for a highly ambitious assembly of the men in Derry.

This explosive sweep of people will anchor the film. The list features both those born and raised on the Bogside – as it became known in the late 1960s – and those who were domiciled in St. Columb's (on scholarships) from other parts of the province. All are contemporaries and many of them have remained in contact since their schooldays. Interviews will thus answer each other and augment individual contributions. Apart from surface similarities of creed and background, there is much in these men that points to a deeper unity – which is the main contention of the film; namely, that this generation is unique and distinct as a result of its time and place.

However, beneath the surface, there are differences between the backgrounds of the boys that are equally rich and will yield much. One such difference is the unequivocal stance Seamus Deane's family had against the policing agents in the North; this is recorded beautifully in his memoir of his childhood years, *Reading in the Dark*. In contrast, the story of Phil Coulter, whose father was a Catholic who served in the Royal Ulster Constabulary, is equally agonising in its tale of entangled loyalties.

Seamus Heaney's life trajectory, arriving in school as the eldest of a big rural family, is likewise in direct contrast to the life of James Sharkey or John Hume, who grew up in a sinisterly cordoned off city where the surge of Catholics against the unionist state was inchoate.

While this documentary explores the childhoods of the contributors exclusively in Derry and in St. Columb's, the subsequent happenings in the lives of the men do bear some examining to illuminate how they now regard their childhoods. For instance, John Hume has lived almost his entire life in Derry. His reflections on growing up there are naturally informed by the gradual transformation of the area into a more habitable residential area, whereas the other contributors, who left the area after graduating from St. Columb's, tend to look at their past in frozen frames, sharply in focus.

It is inevitable that stories of intimidation will feature. Again, the sense of having been hemmed-in and targeted (particularly on August 12th) is more prominent among city-dwellers. These are pungent stories and will make for compelling viewing.

Two musicians' work are obvious choices when it comes to picking music for this film: Phil Coulter and Paul Brady. An album made by Andy Irvine and Paul Brady, eponymously titled, made in 1976 is one possibility. This includes such songs as 'The Streets of Derry' and 'Autumn Gold'. The latter touches on themes of decay and renewal, memory and sorrow, which will run through this entire film.

The other artist is Phil Coulter and, in particular, his poignant song, 'The Town I Loved So Well'. It would provide an entry to a discussion of his father's role in policing in, many would say, a deeply biased police force. It would also be a cue to hear John Hume who has sung this song to Phil Coulter's piano accompaniment in the past.

Music will permeate this film, with score music as background to short readings from Seamus Heaney's work. One of his early poems, 'Mid-Term Break', recalls his waiting in the college sickbay to go home for a family funeral. The author reading this poem while the camera films the sickbay recreates the atmosphere of boarding school superbly. (We have been in touch with the school and had an enthusiastic response from them.) Seamus Deane's work that reflects on their Derry schooling is equally revealing and poignant.

Photography

Headlines and captions will be used from periodicals (especially the *Derry Journal* of the day) to chart the success of this generation of Catholics, from their leaving school through to their graduation from universities like Queen's. We will also use old school journals and the archival material of 'The Boys'. There will be a focus on opinions of local people on their progress. In addition, the film will feature stills about the educational atmosphere of the time, including perceptions of educators (sometimes faux educators) like the Gaelic lovers of the day.

Stills of working class Derry during the 1940s that appear in *The Field Day Review 2* (ed. Seamus Deane), show the beginnings of the labour movement; men and women on street corners, crestfallen, and unemployed; angry union members shaking their fists before an indifferent employer at a work rally.

This is the story of the first generation to receive mass secondary education in Derry in the middle of the last century that made the school of St. Columb's world-famous. Interviews, music and conflicting ideas will combine to make this documentary a valuable addition to Irish history.

This is a history that has yet to find visual expression. We have gathered together an exciting range of people, well-known for their work in their respective fields. Audiences will not be so aware of their common background and their shared identity, having come of a particular era. This film will demonstrate that identity through their own voices. The strength and perseverance that they have shown on the world stage – two participants have earned Nobel Prizes – were in embryo during their school days. This film will be a revelation to people on both sides of the religious divide and to people much further afield. While atrocities against Catholics have been well documented, fewer commentators have remarked on the fact that Northern Irish Catholics had one distinct advantage over their counterparts in the Republic: namely, that they were beneficiaries of an education system that was instrumental in lifting them out of their oppressed state.

The Documentary

The opening of the documentary shows the front of St. Columb's school. There are boys shuffling around the yard in school uniform. The shot is done in sepia.

Cut to a long shot of the river Foyle and then to the houses of the Bogside. Cut to a clear colour, modern-day camera shot. This is the opening of the film proper: an overview of the city. Aerial shots show a long shot of the River Foyle, the fastest flowing river in Europe. There are shots of Craigavon Bridge, which is the scene of several stories of this documentary. It leads directly on to a hill, ascending up centre. The diamond at the centre of the town evokes many traditions: St. Columb's Cathedral, one of the oldest post-reformation Anglican churches extant, is just above it. Then to the houses of the Bogside. Images that echo Coulter's 'In the early mornin/the shirt factory horn/called women from Creggan, the Moor and the Bog'.

The sequence builds with more images. Aerial footage of Derry, a divided town: the Protestant citadel and place of the Siege of Derry; and outside predominantly Catholic terraced housing estates that form areas such as the Bogside and Creggan. Derry is the only walled town in Ireland. Its geography is set in even sharper relief when viewed from the air, from a camera mount in our helicopter.

Footage of the local halls and churches. Rostrum shots of memorabilia and school photographs.

Voice-over begins:

> 'Derry is a city with a long history of divide, reaching back to the seventeenth century. For hundreds of years, the Catholic minority lived on the fringes of the city, downtrodden and isolated ...'

As the camera focuses on paintings of 'The Siege of Derry', there is a feeling that the town was a citadel. Pictures on the walls of the Freemasons museum of 'The Siege of Derry'. This is intended to match our telling of the history of the town.

> 'Since the Treaty of 1921 which partitioned Ireland, conditions of the Catholic minority deteriorated to a level that could scarcely be endured. Even so, one of the advantages of living under the British system – education – developed while everything else decayed. This is the story of eight men, born around WW II, who have made an enormous impact on Ireland and the world.'

All the while, a voice-over tells the history of Derry town. The narrative leads up to the point when, in the late 1930s and 1940s, the generation whose story this film tells was born.

Visual Script: The Boys of St. Columb's Treatment

Interview 1. Seamus Deane, Professor of English Literature at Notre Dame, Indiana; author of Reading in the Dark.

Interviewee explains that going to school was a novel idea to his parents – and an idea they believed in. There were few jobs in Derry anyway – you might as well have stayed at school. Deane explains the pressures Catholic children were under to conform to a British reading of history. He speaks of the Irish language being used as a political weapon; the kindness of some priests who taught; the haughtiness of some other members of the clergy. Footage of the local halls and churches. Rostrum shots of his memorabilia and school photographs.

Shots of the Docks. Camera roves and finds murals of today, magnifies the messages written on them. Cut to the Bogside of Deane's youth. The idea is to show, visually, how occupations echoed class so distinctly in Derry. Deane's eminence as a Notre Dame Professor is set in contrast to his humble origins which he has never forgotten. This is teased out in interview. His disembodied voice talks us through the strife and triumphs of areas around the Bogside of Derry. Those shots parallel the scenes depicted in Deane's novel, which was short-listed for the Booker Prize.

Interview 2. Phil Coulter, Musician and son of a Catholic RUC officer.

Interview delves into the civil strife that was mounting in Derry during his childhood. Interviewee expands on stories of his upbringing and how he was, by turns, stigmatised and envied by his peers on account of his father's occupation. Interviewee speaks of the trials his father faced from an adult's point of view, distilled by the years. Interviewee recounts the contrast between the prevailing attitudes at St. Columb's towards the RUC and those of his household. The trauma that that general hostility caused him as a teenager which prompted him to look into himself for answers at an earlier age than would otherwise have been the case. His terrace house nonetheless containing a piano. He speaks of his embracing of music.

(Music – 'The Town I Loved So Well' plays).

Explains some of the sorrow of growing up as the son of a policeman. His slowly growing towards a consciousness that civil unrest would be the only way to bring about reform. The second half of the interview takes place outside. Coulter recounts the changing face of Derry City.

We follow the camera from Coulter's home place to Phil's father's place of work. Shots from the Bogside, following inside the walled town. Now we follow in a rapid point-of-view shot to the end gate of the town – a school boy's short-cut. Just outside the walls and down Bishop Street to St. Columb's.

Stills of RUC stations then; and shots of police stations now. We follow the camera from Coulter's home place to his father's place of work.

Interview 3. Eamonn McCann, activist and journalist.

Interviewee tells of how his father was deeply involved in the political scene of the day. He explains how he first encountered left-wing ideas at home and how they were grafted on to the predicament of Derry Catholics in his own thinking. Recounts how his father and Seamus Deane's father were best friends. Although a few years younger than Deane, he tells of how he educated Deane into mildly revolutionary thinking on the football pitch at St. Columb's. Scenes of the St. Columb's football fields, located some distance from the school.

Reconstruction: Two young boys are waiting around outside a football field after a game. One, the younger, is holding forth on how Catholics are the proletariat and that the gerrymandering of votes is intolerable. The older listens attentively but his mind returns to football at the end of the monologue.

Camera shots: The church of St. Columb's and religious iconography around the school and Derry.

McCann Interview (continued):

Interviewee speaks about the dominant role the church played in the lives of his people during the 1940s and 1950s. He speaks of his parents' relationship with the church. Rather than being tied with the state of Britain, the church looked towards the Republic for spiritual solidarity. McCann's misgivings about the role the clergy played in his childhood. Haunting tales of beatings for the slightest (or imagined) error at school. Footage of the interior of the school.

McCann recalls why he studied Greek and not French in St. Columb's. He was sitting in the study hall when a priest came around to ask which language he had chosen. He asks, 'Which language do you do if you want to become a priest?' 'You do Greek, McCann', the priest says irately. Trotskyite McCann solemnly says, 'I'll do Greek, then Father'.

Stills of Mossbawn and Bellaghy. Footage of the Heaney home place. Shots of present day Mossbawn. Seamus Heaney reads the last three verses of his poem, 'The Singer's House'.

Interview 4. Seamus Heaney, Nobel Prize laureate, 1995; alumnus of St. Columb's.

Interviewee tells of being the first of nine children born on a farm in County Derry. His teachers in primary school encouraged him to go further with his schooling, so when he won a scholarship to go to St. Columb's his parents supported the idea of his going to boarding school. He speaks of the dormitory and the loneliness of first year. He recounts meeting Seamus Deane (quoting a poem on the subject) with whom he exchanged 'svelte dictions'. Highlights the multifarious differences between being a day-pupil and a boarder. Tells stories of eccentric Latin teachers. Identifies growing discontent in the city and the surprise this was to him, coming from the country. Heaney recalls Phil and Joe Coulter in 'The Real Names'. 'Wise Joe' is 'Good Banquo' – they acted together in the school Christmas play. Deane asks indirectly, by reading from his bildungsroman (p. 91). 'And the priest would ask, under what conditions would you say so, Heaney. And Heaney would reply, "Under the conditions imposed by the question, Father".'

Reconstruction 2. A group of boys in a classroom learning Latin. The priest who is teaching them Horace's Odes grows exasperated at their inability to grasp the subject. He exclaims, 'cannot you see?' Then he moves towards the window and begins to weep for a while. The boys covertly giggle.

Heaney Interview (continued).

Tells of the difficulty of being back at home during summer, feeling guilty about 'shirking' from farm responsibilities. Speaks of further distance he puts between himself and his people on leaving St. Columb's and going 'up to Belfast' for university. Reads from his poem, 'Mid-

Term Break', which highlights this distance due to his being 'away at school'. Explains how he begins to write verse about his home only after wrestling for a long time with the preconception that verse was an urban discipline and had nothing to do with people like him. His unlearning much of what he learned by rote at St. Columb's. Contrast his words to-day with letters he wrote as a boarder. They are read by the voice-over as the camera re-visits the parts of the college to which they refer. Heaney's letters have never been published. This is therefore original material. Background music and also access to Heaney's moving reading of Yeats's 'What Then?' – a poem that reflects on boyhood plans: 'His chosen comrades thought at school/He must grow a famous man ... The work is done/Grown old he thought/According to my boyish plan ...'

Heaney reflects on the transformation he underwent during his time at St. Columb's. He started out a small, shivering eleven year old, too distraught with homesickness to eat his tuck; he ended up Head Prefect of what was to become the biggest Catholic boys' school in Europe. Heaney: 'The older I get, the more I realise how deeply my six years as a boarder affected me.'

Cut to a shot of the stone monument outside the school which reads:

'As we open a new page, we all think of the teachers who helped us to the bottom of all those ones we filled with our writing in St. Columb's and we rejoice that we have shared in the great la-bour of learning which the school continues to represent. Each character formed on each line of each exercise book by pupils in the past, repeats the penwork of the great scribe and poet who is our patron. The many lives lived and the many letters formed are part of one great work.' – Seamus Heaney.

Camera shots: The Inishowen peninsula, cliffs and the sea, a collec-tion of small houses. Cut to the home of James Sharkey.

Interview 5. James Sharkey, alumnus of St. Columb's; Ambassador to Switzerland since July 2007.
Interviewee explains the atmosphere in the city of Derry when he was growing up. His romantic view of Donegal was fed by the occa-sional visits out of town to County Donegal – and his love of Gaelic

culture proceeded from these visits. Shots of Donegal and the border that signaled entering 'The Free State' territory. He speaks of his fear of the RUC when growing up. He explains how rising tensions in the 1960s were brokered in St. Columb's. He reflects on the state of Northern Ireland then, and how things had developed since the partitioning of the country towards the culmination of the civil rights movement. Footage of the civil rights campaign. Describes the conditions of living in Derry at the time. Describes what going to university in Dublin was like, after his intellectual formation at St. Columb's.

Music: 'The Streets of Derry'. Montage of teenagers on the streets. Banners, slogans, murals and protest. Footage of Bloody Sunday and the attack on the British Embassy in Dublin the following day.

Interview 6. Paul Brady, musician and St. Columb's alumnus.

Interviewee is a counterpart to James Sharkey's narrative. They were roommates at UCD. He recalls his disenchantment with the ghastly unreality of the North of Ireland of his youth and how it inspired the quiet timbre of some of his tunes. He shares with James Sharkey a love of Donegal and he elaborates on his long-standing relationship with Gaoth Dobhair. He speaks of his homesickness when he first arrived at school. He speaks of emerging into a liberal Dublin and seeing the contrast to the Derry of his adolescence. Brady reads from and comments on poems he published in the school journal. He remembers the arc of his creativity and its relation with the college.

Interview 7. John Hume, Nobelist, 1995; St. Columb's alumnus.

Interviewee tells of his passionate involvement with Northern politics stemming from his schooldays. He was encouraged to 'go on' in education by priests and other teachers. He became one of the first students from his area to earn a university degree, at Maynooth in 1960. Describes his lifelong relationship with his school, his locale and the Bogside. He reminisces about how education used to be for them: rigorous and violent. He talks about the 'Afrikaner mind set of the unionists: their discriminating had the objective of protecting their identity'.

Brief archival shots of activism in the 1960s in South Africa. Cut to shots of activism on Derry's Bogside to show how they were related.

Shots of other towns in Northern Ireland. He talks of his emerging from the Bogside, canvassing and traveling in other parts of the province and seeing that the Bogside was one of the most discriminated parts of Northern Ireland. His graduate thesis focused on how the economies of Derry and Strabane were stifled by the border. His early involvement with the co-operative movement. He reflects on the importance that the Eleven Plus exam had on the history of the college.

Return interview, Seamus Deane.

Interviewee recounts a sort of 'transition year' that both he and Heaney and a few others had, after they had won scholarships to university. The English teacher, Sean B. O'Kelly, left an indelible mark on him from those days – explains how O'Kelly enthused, and imbued students with a love of the subject.

A reading from *Reading in the Dark*:
The scene is set in the classroom and is read by its author.

Return interview, John Hume.

He also remembers Sean B. O'Kelly fondly and recounts more anecdotes of his inspirational teaching.

CODA

John Hume singing 'The Town I loved so Well', accompanied by Phil Coulter. A sweep of images of the changing face of Derry down through the decades; images previously used in the documentary are used here as montage.

Return interview, John Hume.

An extended comment on the state of Derry city and St. Columb's in today's political climate.

Footage from DVDs of school plays. Boys like Phil Coulter and Seamus Heaney acted in plays such as these.

Cut to shots of fragments of ecclesiastical Latin on the College's church windows. The great imposing four-storied proud facade of the College. Fade up to icons of Christ and the apostles. Photography of murals on the gable ends of Bogside. Contrast with murals of a bygone day in the Bogside.

Photography of the interviewees receiving their Alumni awards from the school. A few words of praise for 'The Boys of St. Columb's' from the present day school president, Father Eamon Martin.

Shot of the school from an artist's perspective at the end of the nineteenth century. This leads into the voice-over, summarising the history of the school – from an ecclesiastic training school through to a conventional secondary school, a shift that was heralded by the 1947 Education Act.

Sign on the wall of St. Columb's school library today: 'Today a reader, tomorrow a leader.'

Each interviewee ponders the impact that their time at St. Columb's had on their lives. They remember the factors that have been permanent.

Stills of alumni receiving their awards from St. Columb's. Fade to close.

'Autumn Gold' plays with the credits.

Credits

Pages 28, 40, 95 – 'Seeking the Kingdom' by J.J.M. Madden and Thomas Madden (privately published)

Page 56 – 'The Gaeltacht' by Seamus Heaney (from *Electric Light*, reproduced by kind permission of Faber and Faber)

Page 57 – 'Ministry of Fear' by Seamus Heaney (from *North*, reproduced by kind permission of Faber and Faber)

Page 66 – 'Mid-Term Break' by Seamus Heaney (from *Death of a Naturulist*, reproduced by kind permission of Faber and Faber)

Page 67 – 'Bodies and Souls' by Seamus Heaney (from *Electric Light*, reproduced by kind permission of Faber and Faber)

Page 68 – 'The Canon or Expectation' by Seamus Heaney (from *The Haw Lantern*, reproduced by kind permission of Faber and Faber)

Page 116 – 'In the Town I Loved So Well', words and music by Phil Coulter (reproduced by kind permission of Phil Coulter and Four Seasons Music)

Page 147 – 'Alumnus Illustrissimus' by Seamus Heaney (reproduced by kind permission of the author)

Page 173 – 'The World Is What You Make It', composed by Paul Brady (reproduced by kind permission of Paul Brady and Hornall Brothers Music)

Page 174 – 'Knowbody Knows', composed by Paul Brady (reproduced by kind permission of Paul Brady and Hornall Brothers Music)

The publisher and author apologise if any permissions were inadvertently omitted and will correct any errors in subsequent editions.

About the Author

Maurice Fitzpatrick was born in Ireland in 1981. He graduated from Trinity College Dublin. In 2004, he was the recipient of the Ministry of Education of Japan scholarship to enable his research on the life and work of Lafcadio Hearn. Since 2007, he has been a lecturer in English at Keio University, Tokyo. He has published articles on Kurosawa's cinematic interpretation of Shakespeare, on the novels of Colm Tóibín and travel journalism. He also has interviewed many writers on their work.

In 2008 he wrote and co-produced *The Boys of St. Columb's*, an RTÉ/BBC documentary film which premiered in Galway Film Fleadh in July 2009 and subsequently screened at the LA Irish Film Festival. In 2010 he will conduct a lecture circuit of the USA and Canada under the auspices of Boston College.

For more information, visit www.mauricefitzpatrick.org.

To purchase the DVD of *The Boys of St Columb's* film, visit www.amazon.co.uk.

Index